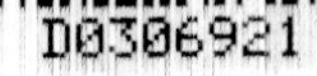

traditional breads

for your breadmaker

KAREN SAUNDERS

traditional breads

for your breadmaker

KAREN SAUNDERS

First published in Great Britain in 2004

1 3 5 7 9 10 8 6 4 2

First published by Ebury Press
Random House, 20 Vauxhall Bridge Road, London SW1V 2SA

Random House Australia (Pty) Limited
20 Alfred Street, Milsons Point, Sydney, New South Wales 2061, Australia

Random House New Zealand Limited
18 Poland Road, Glenfield, Auckland 10, New Zealand

Random House South Africa (Pty) Limited
Endulini, 5A Jubilee Road, Parktown 2193, South Africa

The Random House Group Limited Reg. No. 954009

www.randomhouse.co.uk

A CIP catalogue record for this book is available from the British Library.

Designer and Art Director: Penny Stock
Photographer: William Davis
Props stylist: Annie Rigg
Food stylist: Annie Rigg

ISBN 009190043 3

Papers used by Ebury Press are natural, recyclable products made from wood grown in sustainable forests.

Printed and bound in Singapore by Tien Wah Press

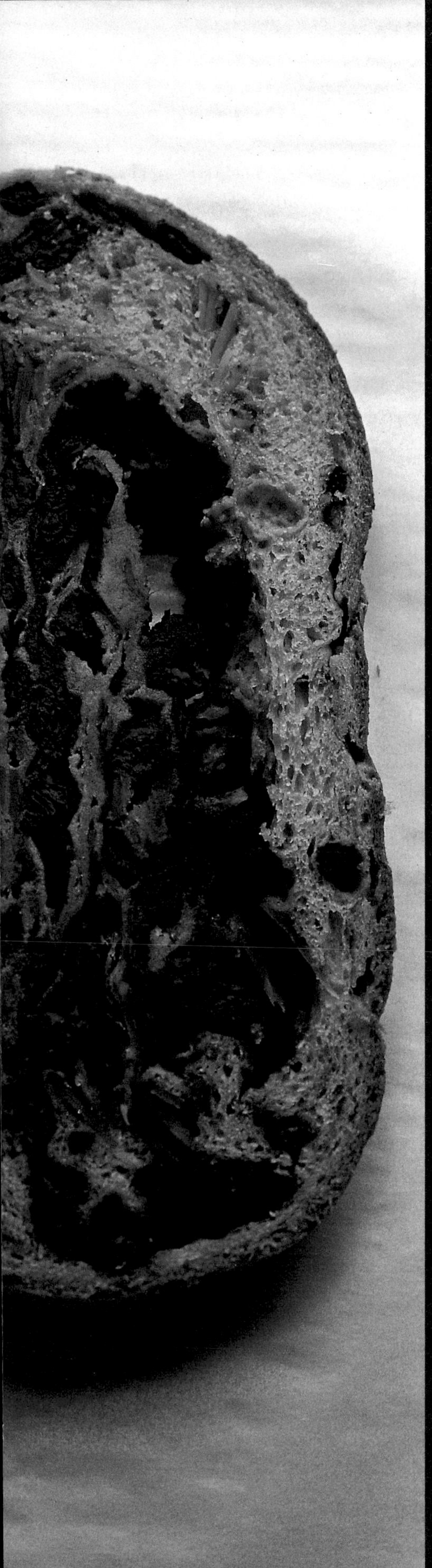

contents

introduction

Bread has come a long way since the first flat loaves, made from coarse meal and water, were baked on a stone over an open fire. Today, our shops are filled with an endless selection of breads with different tastes and textures. Like most of us, I've been overwhelmed with the wonders of continental loaves, of focaccia and pain rustique, calzone and bruschetta, firstly marvelling in their availability at our supermarkets and then rejoicing when I found I could make them equally well at home using my breadmaker.

But what of British bread, I wondered? Where do our traditional loaves sit in the international top ten? I'm afraid that here we've become a forgotten nation; and, I admit that, apart from the odd Chelsea Bun and a few others, I'd largely overlooked our native baking myself. Take a moment to consider the phrase 'traditional British bread' and what it means to you. I remember my grandfather's shopping trips from his farm on the Ashdown Forest. I must have been quite young but can still picture his huge wicker shopping basket. Apart from humbugs, inside would always be cheese with rind wrapped in greaseproof paper, some of that lovely rolled butter and a huge cottage loaf. I can picture him skillfully cutting it into slices with the bread knife he would sharpen on the stone that was his front door step. This bread was really something quite special.

I recall too that, as a child living in rural Berkshire, our weekly shopping trip included a visit to the bakers to buy crusty split tin loaves. I cursed them at the time, wishing that I too could have sliced bread like my friends from school instead of sandwiches made from large unwieldy slices topped with a thick dark crust. I don't remember wishing for packaged bread for very long though: even as children we soon realised our baker's bread promised both superior taste and texture over the pre-sliced, polythene-wrapped alternatives. Looking back, despite my childish tribulations, I'm so grateful for this unlikely introduction to good quality, locally produced bread.

I can't remember my first teacake, doughnut or muffin which suggests that these were things I did not sample until much later in life. This makes me wonder how many children today will have eaten a cookie or an American muffin yet never tried Malt Loaf or a Bath Bun? Is this because our tastes are now so international? Maybe. But I also suspect that many recipes have been lost in the generations, squashed under polythene-wrapped mass-produced buns, cakes and breads.

So what of the world of British bread, I wondered. I knew there had to be more to it than tea cakes and English muffins. So I set off on a new journey and discovered that there was, in fact, a forgotten collection of British recipes. In *The Breadmaker Bible* I showed how easy it was to make bread for every occasion and now I'm taking breadmakers on a new adventure. Our journey takes us all around Britain from Cornwall to the Cairngorms and over the Irish Sea. I've baked Bath Buns and Farls, discovered regional diversity in classics like Gingerbread and Oatcakes, and cast my net far and wide adapting recipes not only for traditional loaves, but for teacakes, buns and batters. The breadmaker can save us so much time and effort with this kind of recipe. So, in addition to the cakes and breads you'd expect, this book contains recipes for the yeast batters that make mouthwatering favourites like fritters, crumpets and pancakes to name just a few.

But this book is not a trip along memory lane or an historical account of British baking. It's a modern adaptation of British classics and a new lifeline for many recipes facing extinction! I've given traditional recipes a contemporary twist; sharing with you a quick and crafty new way to make crumpets and how to give a tasty dough casing to the classic pasties and Eccles cakes. I've created new recipes, too, with the finest local ingredients that I've discovered along the way. The increasing success of farmers' markets and our willingness to purchase food locally from small producers and hunt out new, interesting ingredients is to be embraced. So, I've included recipes that use regional specialities and local ingredients in new contemporary British loaves, giving you the freedom to experiment with specialities from your area. Enjoy breads made with delicacies like Hampshire's peppery watercress, our native crops of oats and barley, British honey and our famous Scottish whisky, not to mention the loaves I have created using the rich and juicy fruits from our nation's orchards and, of course, the finest British cheese.

Now it's true to say that some of the traditional bread recipes would have been baked on a griddle, cooked on a stone or boiled on a range – but with a little modern magic and common sense I'll show how these recipes can be easily made in today's kitchen with help, of course, from the breadmaker. The result, I think, is a wonderful marriage of old and new, with recipes perfect for beginners and experienced cooks alike – so open your eyes, plug in your breadmaker and follow my voyage of discovery unravelling the mouthwatering world of British bread.

HOW TO USE YOUR BREADMAKER

Using a breadmaker to make bread is, in itself, an education. Whether you've made bread previously or you've never mixed dough in your life, I can guarantee that using a breadmaker will mean you'll have to start learning from scratch.

I can't say strongly enough how important it is to learn the basics well, particularly before you try more advanced breadmaker recipes. Read the instructions and the tips and hints in this book and in your manufacturer's handbook and try out the basic loaves several times. Listen to your breadmaker as it works, lift the lid and look at the dough during the mixing cycle, feel it as it's mixing and kneading and you'll soon learn how to correct any mistakes before it's too late.

I'd recommend buying a good basic all-round breadmaker cookbook like the companion titles to this one, *The Complete Bread Machine Cookbook* and *The Breadmaker Bible*. They will guide you through the stages of breadmaking in a breadmaker, ensuring that you save on disappointments and frustration and get the best from your machine.

There are some golden rules to remember when making any breadmaker recipes and I've included the most important ones below.

Measure Carefully

It may sound obvious but this is extremely important. Always use the plastic spoon provided to measure tablespoons and teaspoons and NEVER use domestic spoons as their sizes vary enormously. Whether you choose to measure by cups or by scales, be consistent – never measure some of the ingredients in a cup and others on the scales. As with all recipes choose metric or imperial measures – don't mix the two. I'm a big fan of electronic kitchen scales as these are a quick and easy way to measure both dry and wet ingredients and are very precise.

Choose the Right Yeast

Despite confusing terminology in many manufacturers' handbooks, the only yeast to use in a breadmaker is the instant or fast-acting dried yeast (also called easy-bake yeast). This yeast is available in sachets as well as larger packets, which are more convenient if you bake everyday. Follow the storage and use-by information on the packet carefully and don't try to save partially-used sachets for next time – the yeast will become inactive and your bread will not rise.

The Right Order

Machine manufacturers request that the ingredients are added in a particular order and this is an extremely important piece of advice. Doing this means that the flour acts as a buffer between the yeast and the wet ingredients, ensuring that the yeast does not activate until you are ready to make the loaf. This is especially important when you use the timer and for programmes with a delayed start.

In this book I've added the wet ingredients first, then the flour and finally the yeast. Some machines request that the yeast goes in first and the wet ingredients last, in which case you can simply reverse the order in which the ingredients are added to the bucket by reading the list from the bottom to the top.

Choose the Right Programme

Always select the programme stated in the recipe. Be aware that rapid and turbo programmes are not suitable for all recipes.

If your machine does not have a cake programme, you can mix the cake recipes by hand and then choose the 'bake' programme for cooking. If you need to select the baking time, consult your manufacturer's handbook for guidance. I usually find the total quantity of flour is a good indicator of how long the cake will need. Manufacturer's cake recipes can then be used as a guide.

Test cakes as if you are baking by conventional methods. Insert a skewer into the middle and if it comes out clean, the cake is cooked. Most machines let you adjust the timer and add extra minutes to the baking cycle, so you can run the cycle until your cake is cooked completely.

Create the Right Environment

It may seem strange but where you keep your breadmaker can greatly influence the results of your baking. Keep your machine in a dry and draught-free place at a comfortable room temperature – never outside, or in the garage and never in direct sunlight, or next to the hob or oven. Ensure there is ample space around and above your machine for air to circulate and that the vents are not obstructed. Take care when your machine is baking as the surfaces can get quite hot and steam can puff out of the

air vents. Also, you should always be aware that sudden changes in the weather or your central heating can affect the results of your baking. Flour will be naturally drier in the summertime than in the damp winter months and so you may well need to add slightly more liquid. If your central heating is on at a high temperature, you may again need to add more liquid. A sudden heat wave may mean that your bread does not rise as well because high humidity can affect the yeast's performance.

Look After your Breadmaker

I know it's tempting, but don't put your breadmaker's bucket in the dishwasher as it will damage the paddle mechanism. Follow your manufacturer's instructions for cleaning the machine. Never use metal utensils in it as they will scratch the non-stick surface.

If your paddle gets stuck in the bottom of your bread, carefully remove it with a pair of plastic kitchen tongs, taking care not to damage the non-stick surface of the paddle, or your bread. It's worth noting that most manufacturers sell extra paddles and buckets. (For manufacturers' details, see page 172.)

Variety is the Spice of Life

Finally, remember that you are making homemade bread and that every loaf will be slightly different in colour, texture and shape, unlike commercially-made goods. Enjoy the fresh-baked smells, the delicious natural tastes and, of course, the fact that they are completely unique!

BREADMAKING INGREDIENTS

For thousands of years, bread has been made from a mixture of flour, salt and water. The composition of this flour would depend very much on the region. In more temperate climates, where wheat grew freely, the bread was made from this grain. But in harsh landscapes, where hardier crops like oats and rye were more prevalent, dwellers would have made a very different looking loaf.

With the agricultural reforms in the mid-18th century, the work of pioneers like Coke of Norfolk and Jethro Tull meant that far more land was turned over to wheat. Gradually wheat crops took prevalence over the hardier varieties of oats, barley and rye. The availability of wheat flour led to a more refined loaf of bread and this was the beginning of the loaves we all know and love today.

With a wealth of flour and flavouring options available to us, we have everything we need to make an endless variety of loaves. But good basic ingredients are essential for success, so it's worth recapping on how these can be used to vary the taste and texture of our bread.

Wheat Flours

For the best bread, high-protein flour made from 'hard' or 'strong' wheat should be used. When you knead dough made from strong flour, the protein from the flour develops into gluten. Gluten is the elastic substance that forms the mesh-like structure which encapsulates the carbon dioxide bubbles given off by the fermenting yeast. It is the gluten structure that allows dough to develop into the light and airy texture of fresh cooked bread.

Common British Bread Flours

STRONG WHITE BREAD FLOUR

The bran and germ are removed from the flour during milling, producing flour which will make light and airy white bread.

VERY STRONG WHITE BREAD FLOUR

This premium white bread flour is blended from the finest hard wheat varieties. These are generally from Canada and North America and they produce a flour super-high in gluten. It can be used whenever a recipe calls for strong white bread flour and will generally help to give a better volume and lighter results. This flour is also particularly useful for giving improved rise and texture to bread made with a blend of flours that are naturally low in gluten like wholemeal, rye and barley.

STRONG WHOLEMEAL FLOUR

Quite simply, wholemeal means that the whole grain (including the germ and bran) has been used to make the flour. In technical terms, wholemeal flour is said to be of 100% extraction and is, consequently, a useful source of B vitamins, calcium, iron and fibre.

However, for breadmaker users it's not all good news. The bran in wholemeal flour reduces the effectiveness of gluten during baking. So bread made with wholemeal flour will never rise as high as bread made without the germ and bran and will also be much denser than its white equivalent. The presence of bran in the flour also means that the dough will absorb much more liquid, so more water is needed when wholemeal flour is used. If you want the benefits of wholemeal flour, therefore, I'd always recommend using a 50:50 blend for best results (50% strong white, or very strong white flour and 50% strong wholemeal).

WHOLESOME WHITE VERY STRONG BREAD FLOUR
This innovative blend of strong white bread flour and a new strong white wheat wholemeal flour offers the best of both worlds. Used in a breadmaker, it will give a wonderfully light loaf with a creamy coloured interior that contains all the goodness of wholemeal flour.

STRONG BROWN FLOUR
Brown flour differs from wholemeal in that it has had 10% of the grain's bran removed during milling, i.e. it is of 90% extraction. Brown flour is high in nutrients and will still absorb slightly more liquid than white flour. However, it will produce a noticeably lighter loaf than wholemeal and so, unlike regular wholemeal, it is possible to use 100% strong brown flour and make excellent loaves.

COUNTRY GRAIN STRONG BROWN BREAD FLOUR
This flour is made from strong brown flour enhanced with malted wheat flakes. You may also find that this flour is called malted wheat grain or granary.

SOFT GRAIN STRONG WHITE BREAD FLOUR
This is strong white flour with cracked wheat and rye grains which add fibre to the flour and also give the bread an interesting texture and additional 'bite'.

RYE FLOUR
Rye has been cultivated in Britain for centuries. It was often sown together with wheat to make a crop known as 'maslin' (mixed). Rye was used in many traditional British recipes but as wheat became more prominent later in the 18th century, its use diminished.

Rye actually has a good gluten content but its gluten is of a different nature to that of wheat and it is, unfortunately, far inferior in terms of breadmaking. Rye is, therefore, best used in conjunction with wheat flour. The combination will give a delicious tangy flavour and close texture to the bread.

BARLEY FLOUR

Barley has been used in bread for centuries but it is low in gluten and therefore, on its own, is unsuitable for use in a breadmaker. However, when blended with wheat flours in small quantities it can add an extra earthy dimension to bread. Barley flour is grey-brown in colour and will give a darker crumb to a loaf when mixed with white bread flour.

OATMEAL

As another traditional British grain, oats are used in breadmaking either as a coarse meal or finely ground into flour. When mixed with strong flour in the breadmaker, oats can add an extra dimension to loaves. You'll see I've used the various grades of oatmeal in traditional recipes throughout this book.

RICE FLOUR

Historically, bread made with rice has been held in high esteem, praised for taste, texture and its keeping qualities. Rice was originally used as a bread ingredient to moisten the bread and to make the dough go further, in the same way potatoes were used. Rice was frequently added to recipes in the form of cooked whole grains, a coarse meal or as flour.

CORNMEAL (or MAIZE MEAL)

Cornmeal is a coarsely ground 'granular' meal made from maize. It's extremely useful for adding to breads to vary colour (it gives a rich yellow tone), flavour and texture.

Yeast

I find it fascinating to think that yeast must have been discovered by accident when a mix of meal and water was left out in a warm place for longer than usual and started to ferment. With the resulting loaf being lighter and more appetising, it didn't take long for fermentation, using naturally occurring air-borne yeast, to become an essential part of breadmaking.

The practice of storing a piece of leaven from the day's dough and keeping it alive for the next batch soon became the routine. Today, bread can still be made in this traditional way, although commercially manufactured yeast allows us much more convenience.

Quite simply, yeast works by feeding on the sugar from the mix and the starch from the flour. Given the right environment of warmth and moisture it will grow, giving off carbon dioxide and alcohol. When this happens in bread dough, the gas bubbles get caught in the mesh-like gluten structure and expand. This causes the dough to rise until the heat of the oven finally kills off the yeast and the starch in the flour sets, holding the shape of the risen loaf.

When baking traditionally you can judge when dough has risen just enough and you can then bake the dough to kill off the yeast. However, in a breadmaker, the timings of the cycles are strictly regulated. This means that the fermentation must be controlled by adding exactly the right amount of yeast to the recipe and also with the use of salt.

Instant or fast-acting dried yeast makes things as simple as they can get, but I can't stress too much the importance of accurate measuring. Always use the measure supplied with your machine, and never household cutlery. Be aware, also, that too many sweet ingredients and other ingredients like onions, garlic and alcohol can inhibit the action of the yeast and make your loaves denser.

Do not use fresh yeast in your breadmaker or traditional dried active yeast (sold in tins) as these are both more suited to baking by traditional methods than to breadmaker baking.

Salt

Salt is an essential ingredient for making loaves in a breadmaker as it helps control the action of the yeast. In addition, salt gives bread a well-rounded flavour while improving the keeping qualities of the loaf. Be aware, though, that salt must be used with care. Too much will kill the yeast and too little will mean that the dough rises out of control.

Sugar

Sugar gives the yeast a boost, helping to ensure adequate fermentation within the limits of the machine's cycle. Sugar can be added in any form including jam, honey, syrup and even fruit concentrates. Be aware, though, that when recipes have many sweet ingredients, the increased amounts of sugar can inhibit the action of the yeast and make a denser loaf.

Liquid

Almost any liquid can be used to bind bread dough. While water is the usual choice, milk, cream, buttermilk or natural yoghurt have all been used traditionally, as well as beer, cold tea, juices and wine. Whatever liquid is used, bear in mind that yeast is heat sensitive and that liquid should be added at the right temperature. Yeast will die if the liquid is too hot or too cold. Most breadmakers will gently heat the dough as it mixes, so don't worry too much about accurately measuring the temperature with a thermometer to the last degree. Simply ensure your ingredients are at room temperature.

Fat

In our low-fat world it's often forgotten that you can add fats like butter and oil to bread to enhance its crumb structure, taste and keeping qualities. Butter, and vegetable fat and oils, can be substituted to vary the flavour to suit your taste. But don't use low fat spreads unless they are designed for baking.

Many of the traditional recipes in this book would have used lard and, of course, you can too. However, in the interests of health, I've used hard white vegetable fat in its place in most of the recipes.

Other Ingredients

Eggs

Eggs have been used for centuries to enrich bread dough. Always use the size of egg stated in the recipe and ensure that they are at room temperature before use.

Eggs are also used in this book to make egg wash, a classic glaze made by whisking a whole egg together with a couple of tablespoons of cold water and a pinch of salt.

Fruit, Nuts, Cheese, Herbs, Spices and other Flavourings

Use your common sense when adding these ingredients. Herbs, spices, seeds and cheese can simply be added with the other dry ingredients. Softer ingredients, like dried or ready-to-eat fruit and nuts, can be added during the second kneading cycle. This will ensure that they retain their shape and will prevent them getting mashed up by the paddle during mixing. Most machines have a 'bleep' to signal when extra ingredients can be added and some models even have a little trap door in the lid that automatically drops the ingredients in at the best time.

Local Specialities

Many of my own recipes in this book use regional specialities like local cheeses. I've listed suppliers for these products, where appropriate, in the back of the book. If, however, you would like to substitute a similar product from your region you can do so as long as you bear in mind the basic principles outlined in this section. Don't exceed the amounts I've stated, as excessive cheese in a recipe, for example, will spoil the loaf.

Cheese is one of the most versatile ingredients for flavouring bread and any cheese can be added to suit your particular taste. If you've chosen a particularly mild cheese like Cheshire or Wensleydale for your loaf, you can enhance the overall flavour further by adding additional cheese as a topping. This is best done by either sprinkling grated or finely crumbled cheese over the bread during the last few minutes of the baking cycle or once the hot loaf has been removed from the tin.

Cheese can also be added as a filling. Why not follow the recipe for Breadmaker Pasties (page 32) and replace the filling with a mix of your favourite cheese, finely chopped spring onions, halved cherry tomatoes and a few fresh herbs? Or, try Lancashire Cheese and Apple Cake (page 100) with your favourite local cheese. If you choose a blue cheese like Stilton, Dorset Blue Vinney or Lanark Blue try also substituting the apples for Conference pears for a delicious combination.

When adding dried fruit and nuts you can substitute varieties according to your taste. Generally dough using 450 g/16 oz/3 cups of flour will take approximately 1 cup of added ingredients. Delicious breads can be made with native British nuts like walnuts and hazelnuts. These are widely available and are excellent in bread, especially if pre-roasted for a few minutes in a hot oven to bring out their flavour. For something unusual why not try cobnuts? They give a well rounded nutty taste and delicious texture. Unlike other nuts, however, cobnuts are sold fresh. Grown in Kent, they are in season between August and October and are available by mail order (suppliers on page 172). Whatever nuts you choose, maximize flavour and texture in your loaf by grinding half quite finely in the food processor and adding the remainder chopped.

Don't forget that the liquid you choose for your loaf has a great influence on its flavour. Try using your local beer, ale, cider or perry. For best results, leave fizzy brews to become flat, or warm them slightly before use. As when drinking, dark stouts have a stronger flavour and lighter beers a mellow tone (try the Rustic Beer Bread on page 44). Cider and perry are particularly good used in cheese-flavoured loaves. Try cider instead of water in Cheddar Cheese and Walnut Bread (page 34) and you're sure to love the results.

right **Porter Cake (page 143)**

the west country

the west country

As Britain's most westerly point, The Isles of Scilly lie 28 miles off the Cornish coast in the Atlantic Ocean. These small islands are the first corner of the triangular peninsula known as the West Country, which encompasses the counties of Cornwall, Devon and Dorset, and includes the city of Bath in Somerset and the rolling downs of Wiltshire and the Cotswold Hills that form the eastern boundary of Gloucestershire. Blessed with the mildest climate in Britain, seas warmed by the Gulf Stream and fertile land, the counties spanning this corner of Britain are a gastronomic delight.

For centuries West Country dwellers throughout Cornwall, Devon and Dorset have enjoyed the bounty of the sea, not only in terms of fishing but also as a link to explore and trade with faraway lands. Early seafarers returned with exotic goods like the spice saffron that is used in two of Cornwall's most famous dishes – Saffron Cake (page 25) and Saffron Buns (page 26).

The fertile pastures of this region make excellent food for cattle and sheep. Indeed, the combination of Cornish cream and Devon butter along with with Cornish Splits and Devonshire Chudleighs (page 30) are the cornerstones of the British cream tea. Cream from Somerset cattle is used for some of our most famous cheese, while in the north of the region Gloucestershire has both its own cheese and 'cheese rolling' – a traditional race involving competitors chasing cheese down a hill.

Spring comes early in the West Country, producing blossom and flowering hedgerows from which bees can feed. It's an important place for honey production with local farm varieties popular throughout the region. Of course, much of the blossom here is from apple trees: the essential ingredient for the famous cider, used in traditional recipes like Somerset Apple Cake (page 28) and Cider Cake with Honey Icing (page 29).

Moving away from the countryside, Somerset is home to the spa city of Bath which has inspired an abundance of traditional breads from Sally Lunns to its namesake Bath Buns – both still available in the city today.

sally lunns

Sally Lunns are arguably Bath's most famous bread and the original recipe remains a closely guarded secret. Having been in existence since before Roman times, Bath has long been famed for the healing powers of its hot springs. In fact, in the 18th century, Bath was Britain's most fashionable resort and consequently the city developed many dishes all of its own, including Sally Lunns. The origins of the bun itself are varied; some say it's named after a girl of the same name, others that it's a corruption of the West Country French, 'Solet-Lune' meaning sun and moon which is a good description of this cake with a flat moon-like top and golden, sunny centre. The Sally Lunn restaurant in Bath prefers the story of Sally Lunn, a young refugee, who arrived in England over 300 years ago and first baked the rich, light round bun. Whichever story you favour, you'll love the taste and texture of these versatile cakes, based on the originals served in Bath. You can choose from a variety of sweet and savoury fillings and toppings, although most books report that the traditional way to enjoy a Sally Lunn is served warm with sweetened whipped cream.

Makes 4

you need

225 ml/8 fl oz/1 cup full cream milk
100 ml/$3^1/_2$ fl oz/$^7/_{16}$ cup melted butter
2 large eggs, beaten
50 g/2 oz/$^3/_{16}$ cup caster sugar
$^1/_2$ tsp salt
450 g/16 oz/3 cups very strong white bread flour
$2^1/_2$ tsp instant or fast-acting dried yeast

to make

Lightly grease a baking tray. Pour the milk, butter and eggs into the breadmaker bucket. Add the sugar and salt and cover the mixture with the flour. Finally, sprinkle the yeast over the top. Fit the bucket into the breadmaker and set to the dough programme. When the cycle is complete, turn the dough out on to a lightly floured surface and knead until smooth. Divide the dough into 4 equally-sized pieces and shape each piece of dough into a flat cake. Put the cakes on to the baking sheet, cover with a tea towel and leave in a warm place to prove until doubled in size. Bake in a preheated oven at 200°C/400°F/gas mark 6 for 15–20 minutes until golden.

wiltshire lardy cake

Lardy cake holds special childhood memories for me – rich and sweet, this moist layered cake was packed with fruit and sugar and came warm from our local bakers. We'd always hurry home from shopping and eat it straight away with our afternoon cup of tea, enjoying its sticky toffee-like texture and crisp brown crust. With the advent of healthy eating, lardy cake may have faded in popularity but it can still be found in good bakeries all over Wiltshire. In my recipe I've used the marginally healthier vegetable fat instead of traditional lard – though either will work well.

you need

275 ml/10 fl oz/1¼ cups water
2 tbsp hard white vegetable fat
1 tsp salt
1 tbsp granulated sugar
450 g/16 oz/3 cups strong white bread flour
2 tsp instant or fast-acting dried yeast

For the filling:

75g/3 oz/1 cup butter, cut into small dice*
75g/3 oz/1 cup hard white vegetable fat, cut into small dice*
100g/3½ oz/¾ cup mixed dried fruit
75g/3 oz/5/16 cup granulated sugar

to make

Lightly grease a Swiss roll tin of 23 cm/9 in x 33 cm/13 in. To make the dough, pour the water into the breadmaker bucket followed by the fat, salt and sugar. Cover the ingredients with the flour and sprinkle the yeast over the top. Fit the bucket into the breadmaker and set to the dough programme. Meanwhile prepare the filling ingredients. Carefully measure out the fats and mix them together with a knife, and then divide the fat mixture into three approximately equal pieces. When the cycle is complete, turn the dough out on to a lightly floured surface and knead until smooth. Roll the dough out into a rectangle about 0.5 cm/¼ in thick. Cover the top two thirds of the rectangle with one third of the filling ingredients; dotting little slices of the fat over the surface and then sprinkling a third of the fruit and sugar mix over. Fold the dough into three, folding the bottom third up and the top third down – like an envelope. Press the edges together to seal. Give the dough a quarter turn, and then roll out as before and repeat the filling and folding process until all the filling ingredients have been added. If the dough gets sticky as you are rolling, simply dust with a little flour, but take care not to add too much or the dough will dry out. Finally roll the dough out to a thickness of about 2.5 cm/1 in and place into the tin. Cover with a tea towel and leave in a warm place for 30 minutes to prove. Score the top of the dough with a knife and bake in a preheated oven at 220°C/425°F/gas mark 7 for 25–30 minutes until crisp and golden.

*When using a cup to measure the fat, first cut the fat into small pea-sized dice and put into the cup. Do not press down. For best results double check your measurement using scales.

bath buns

Dr W. Oliver, founder of Bath's Mineral Water Hospital, made the famous Bath Buns for his rich London patients who visited Bath to take in its healing waters. Unfortunately the Bath Buns were so popular that his patients ate too many of them and consequently undid all the good the Doctor was doing. As a shrewd business man, Dr Oliver decided to invent a better snack for them in the form of a plain biscuit known today as the Bath Oliver. As with many old recipes every version of the Bath Bun recipe varies slightly. I've found references to Bath Buns being topped with a few currants, with saffron in the dough and also with caraway seeds. It's said that the crunchy sugar coating on Bath Buns served today signifies the crushed caraway seed comfits that were used to flavour the buns in former times. These comfits were made by dipping the seeds repeatedly in boiling sugar until they were thickly coated.

Makes 10

you need

For the batter:

100 ml/$3\frac{1}{2}$ fl oz/$\frac{7}{16}$ cup milk

100 ml/$3\frac{1}{2}$ fl oz/$\frac{7}{16}$ cup water

1 tsp sugar

150 g/$5\frac{1}{4}$ oz/1 cup plain flour

$2\frac{1}{2}$ tsp instant or fast-acting dried yeast

For the dough:

2 medium eggs, beaten

3 tbsp melted butter

1 tsp salt

75 g/3 oz/$\frac{5}{16}$ cup caster sugar

300 g/11 oz/2 cups plain flour

100 g/$3\frac{1}{2}$ oz/$\frac{3}{4}$ cup sultanas

50 g/2 oz/$\frac{1}{4}$ cup mixed peel

For the glaze & topping:

1 small egg, beaten

1 tsp caster sugar

1 tbsp water

14 sugar cubes, roughly crushed

to make

Lightly grease a baking tray. To make the batter, mix the milk, water, sugar, flour and yeast together until smooth and leave to ferment in a warm place for 20 minutes until the mixture starts to bubble. Pour the batter into the breadmaker bucket and add the eggs, butter, salt, sugar and flour. Fit the bucket into the breadmaker and set to the dough programme. Add the sultanas and mixed peel according to your manual's instructions, usually at the beginning of the second kneading cycle or when the machine bleeps. When the programme is complete, turn the dough out on to a lightly floured board and knead until smooth. Divide the dough into 10 equally-sized pieces and shape into rounds. Place on the baking sheet, cover with a tea towel and leave in a warm place for 30 minutes to prove. To make the glaze, mix the egg, sugar and water together and brush the mixture over the proved buns. Finally, sprinkle with the crushed sugar cubes. Bake the buns in a preheated oven at 200°C/400°F/gas mark 6 for 12–15 minutes until golden.

the secrets of saffron

Most are surprised to learn that a spice regarded as so exotic today has, in fact, played a significant part in cake and bread recipes for thousands of years in this country. As early as pre-Christian times, Phoenicians were said to have brought saffron to the shores of Cornwall when they came to trade in tin. Cornish cooks quickly found this brightly coloured spice an excellent ingredient, adding both colour and a distinctive flavour to sweet and savoury dishes. In bread making, saffron stamens were often steeped in warm water in a covered jar and the yellow liquor used in the dough that would then take on the golden colour of the saffron. Two of the most famous Cornish saffron recipes are featured here; the classic Saffron Buns and the aromatic Saffron Cake.

cornish saffron cake

Cornwall's most traditional cake is in fact a yeasted tea bread. Serve it simply buttered, try it as toast, or, for a treat, slice it while still warm and top with clotted cream.

you need

175 ml/6 fl oz/$\frac{3}{4}$ cup full cream milk
1 tsp saffron strands
125 ml/4 fl oz/$\frac{1}{2}$ cup melted butter
1 tsp salt
50 g/2 oz/$\frac{3}{16}$ cup caster sugar
Pinch each of ground nutmeg, cinnamon and mixed spice
450 g/16 oz/3 cups plain flour
1$\frac{1}{2}$ tsp instant or fast-acting dried yeast
50 g/2 oz/$\frac{1}{4}$ cup sultanas
50 g/2 oz/$\frac{5}{16}$ cup currants
For the glaze:
1 tbsp full cream milk
2 tsp caster sugar

to make

Put the milk into a saucepan and bring to the boil. Stir in the saffron strands and leave to stand for 30 minutes until the milk is well coloured but still lukewarm. Pour the saffron infusion into the breadmaker bucket together with the butter. Add the salt, sugar and spices and cover the liquid with the flour. Finally, sprinkle the yeast over the top. Fit the bucket into the breadmaker and set to the basic white programme. Add the sultanas and currants according to your manual's instructions, usually at the beginning of the second kneading cycle or when the machine bleeps. Whisk the milk and sugar together to make the glaze and set aside. Once cooked, carefully shake the loaf from the bucket and stand it the right way up on a wire cooling rack. While it is still hot, brush the loaf with the glaze. Leave the bread to cool for at least an hour before cutting and/or removing the paddle if necessary.

cornish saffron buns

These sweet fruit buns are delicately coloured and flavoured with saffron. It is said that they were traditionally served as an Easter delicacy in Cornwall, though I'd say they're too delicious to serve just once a year.

Makes 8–10

you need

1 tsp saffron strands
200 ml/7 fl oz/⅞ cup semi-skimmed milk
2 tbsp water
1½ tsp salt
4 tbsp granulated sugar
150 ml/5 fl oz/¾ cup melted butter
450 g/16 oz/3 cups strong white bread flour
2½ tsp instant or fast-acting dried yeast
75 g/3 oz/½ cup raisins or mixed dried fruit
For the glaze:
1 small egg
2 tbsp semi-skimmed milk

to make

Lightly grease a baking tray. Put the saffron strands and milk into a saucepan and heat slowly until the milk boils, stirring all the time. Remove the pan from the heat and leave to infuse for 30 minutes. Pour the saffron infusion into the breadmaker bucket and add the water, salt, sugar and melted butter. Cover the liquid with the flour and sprinkle the yeast over the top. Fit the bucket into the breadmaker and set to the dough programme. Add the dried fruit according to your manual's instructions, usually at the beginning of the second kneading cycle or when the machine bleeps. When the cycle is complete, turn the dough out on to a lightly floured surface and knead until smooth. Divide the dough into 8–10 equally sized pieces and shape into buns. Put the buns on to the baking sheet, cover with a tea towel and leave in a warm place to prove until doubled in size. To make the glaze, whisk together the egg and milk and brush over the buns. Bake in a preheated oven at 200°C/400°F/gas mark 6 for 15 minutes until golden.

apple traditions

Historically some would place apples as our oldest fruit – remember Adam and Eve! In fact we've been enjoying apples for over 750,000 years. Today our earliest home grown English apples start to appear in mid-summer with the later varieties finishing their harvest in the early winter months. Classic English apple varieties like Bramley, Cox's Orange Pippin and Russet are well known and today, thankfully, several other traditional varieties are also widely available including Beauty of Bath, Jonagold, Winter Wonder and Adam's Pearmain.

Apples have become the subject of much folklore over the centuries and today many festivals are still enjoyed in celebration of this very British crop. In Somerset, the apple harvest runs until November, producing cider from the sweet and juicy varieties. On Christmas Eve it's traditional to enjoy 'Lambs' Wool', a drink made from heated ale and spice that's served with clove-studded roasted apples, nuts and hot cakes. On Twelfth Night, wassailing traditionally took place when farmers and workers blessed their apple trees to ensure a fine crop for the coming summer.

Wassail means 'be healthy'. The ceremony varied by region but in essence it took place after dark and around the best tree in the orchard. Cider was poured over the roots of the tree and pieces of toast or cakes, also soaked in cider, placed in the forks of branches who, representing the spirit of the tree, were also given gifts of bread, cheese and cider.

somerset apple cake

This is a wonderfully moist cake that can also be served as a dessert with thick cream or custard.

you need

450 g/1 lb cooking apples
100 g/$3^{1}/_{2}$ oz/$^{7}/_{16}$ cup very soft butter
175 g/6 oz/$1^{5}/_{8}$ cup light soft brown sugar
2 large eggs beaten
3 tbsp semi-skimmed milk
1 tsp mixed spice
1 tsp ground cinnamon
300 g/11 oz/2 cups self-raising flour
2 tsp baking powder

to make

Peel, core and finely chop the apples. Put the apple into the breadmaker bucket, followed by the other ingredients. Fit the bucket into the breadmaker and set to the cake programme. Once cooked, remove the bucket from the machine and leave the cake to cool for 5 minutes before carefully shaking it from the bucket and standing it the right way up on a wire cooling rack. Serve either warm or cold, with thick cream.

cider cake with honey icing

Cider has a long history in the West Country, and it was after the Norman Conquest of 1066 that cider consumption became popular in England, and orchards became established to produce the apples needed for this new and increasingly popular drink. During medieval times, cider making became an important industry and records show that at this time monasteries were growing apples, making strong, spiced cider and selling it to the public.

Cider making peaked in the 17th century when it was usual for most farms and manors to have their own orchards and cider presses. In the 18th century much was done to improve and standardize cider-making techniques and following this, cider apple orchards were planted in profusion in Somerset and Devon. Cider grew in popularity and in the West it was usual for workers to receive a daily allocation of cider as part of their wages.

Traditional West Country apple varieties like Sweet Alford, Woodbine and Morgan's Sweet are still used for making cider by small, specialist producers who fiercely cherish their secret recipes to preserve the exclusivity of the distinctively flavoured drink.

This light cake has a rich flavour that perfectly combines the apple undertones of cider with the sweetness of honey.

you need

150 ml/5 fl oz/$\frac{5}{8}$ cup Somerset cider
250 g/9 oz/1$\frac{5}{8}$ cups sultanas
2 large eggs, beaten
100 g/3$\frac{1}{2}$ oz/$\frac{1}{2}$ cup soft butter
100 g/3$\frac{1}{2}$ oz/$\frac{5}{8}$ cup light soft brown sugar
225 g/8 oz/1$\frac{1}{2}$ cups plain flour
2 tsp bicarbonate of soda

For the icing:

50 g/2 oz/$\frac{1}{4}$ cup soft butter
50 g/2 oz/$\frac{3}{8}$ cup icing sugar
1 tbsp runny honey
4 tbsp lemon juice

to make

First, soak the sultanas in the cider for 2 hours. To make the cake, pour the soaked sultanas and the remaining cider into the breadmaker bucket. Add the eggs, butter and sugar and cover the mixture with the flour. Finally sprinkle the bicarbonate of soda over the top. Fit the bucket into the breadmaker and set to the cake programme. After a few minutes of the mixing cycle, scrape down the mixture on the sides of the bucket with a plastic spatula to ensure all the ingredients are evenly mixed. When the cycle is complete, remove the bucket from the machine and leave the cake to cool for 5 minutes. Carefully shake the loaf from the bucket, stand it the right way up on a wire cooling rack and leave to cool. To make the icing, beat the butter, sugar, honey and lemon juice together to form a smooth paste. Once the cake is completely cold, cover it with the icing.

cornish splits

The cream tea is the quintessential West Country treat. Cornish Splits are the cornerstone of the Cornish cream tea, served split open with clotted cream and strawberry jam. These light buns are enriched with full cream milk and butter making them the perfect host for rich, sweet fillings. They are also known as 'thunder and lightning' if served with clotted cream and black treacle.

Makes 16

you need

150 ml/5 fl oz/$^5/_8$ cup water
25 g/1 oz/$^1/_8$ cup hard white vegetable fat
50 g/2 oz/$^1/_4$ cup butter
6 tbsp full cream milk
1 tbsp granulated sugar
pinch of salt
450 g/16 oz/3 cups plain flour
2$^1/_2$ tsp instant or fast-acting dried yeast
For the glaze:
1 egg
1 tbsp water
pinch of salt

to make

Lightly grease a baking tray. Put the water, fat, butter and milk into a saucepan and heat gently until the fats have melted. Do not let the mixture boil. Pour the mixture into the breadmaker bucket and leave to cool slightly before adding the sugar, salt and flour. Finally, sprinkle the yeast over the top. Fit the bucket into the breadmaker and set to the dough programme. When the cycle is complete, turn the dough out on to a lightly floured surface and knead until smooth. Divide the dough into 16 equally-sized pieces and shape each piece into a round cake. Put the cakes on to the baking sheet, cover with a tea towel and leave in a warm place to prove until doubled in size. To make the glaze, whisk together the egg, water and salt. Brush over the proved dough and bake in a preheated oven at 200°C/400°F/gas mark 6 for 10–12 minutes until golden. Remove the buns from the baking tray and, if not serving immediately, wrap in a tea towel to keep them warm and soft. Serve with clotted cream and jam.

devonshire chudleighs

Devonshire Chudleighs are made in the same way as Cornish Splits but are smaller. In North Devon these are called 'Cut Rounds' and in south Devon they are known as 'Splits'.
To make Devonshire Chudleighs follow the recipe above but make smaller buns – dividing the dough into 20–24 pieces should produce buns the right size. These will cook quicker than the splits in the recipe above, so I would suggest checking them after 8–10 minutes in the oven.

breadmaker pasties

Cornish Pasties have to be the most famous of all Cornish fare, so how could I not include them in a regional cookbook? I've used a light dough to contain the traditional meat and potato filling, making this recipe a cross between a pasty and a calzone. It is thought that pasties evolved to meet the needs of tin miners who wanted a hearty meal packed in a convenient casing. In order to give the men two courses, Cornish housewives would fill one end with meat and vegetables and the other with a jam or fruit filling. Pasties would be marked with the miner's initials to avoid confusion should they wish to save a corner of the pasty for later or give some to the 'knockers' – the little people of the mines who, according to many miners, caused all kinds of mischief unless placated with a small amount of food!

Makes 4 large pasties

you need

275 ml/10 fl oz/1½ cups water
3 tbsp olive oil
1½ tsp salt
2 tsp granulated sugar
450 g/16 oz/3 cups strong white bread flour
2 tsp instant or fast-acting dried yeast

For the filling:

450g/1 lb rump steak
3 medium potatoes
1 medium onion
salt and black pepper

For the glaze:

1 small egg
3 tbsp semi-skimmed milk

to make

Lightly grease a baking tray. To make the dough, pour the water and oil into the breadmaker bucket, followed by the salt and sugar. Cover with the flour and sprinkle the yeast over the top. Fit the bucket into the breadmaker and set to the dough programme. Just before the end of the dough cycle, prepare the filling ingredients. Slice the steak across the grain into small even-sized pieces, and peel the potatoes and onion and slice them thinly. When the cycle is complete, turn the dough out on to a lightly floured surface and divide into 4 pieces. Roll each piece of dough into a circle about the same thickness as pastry. Cover one half of each circle with a mixture of the filling ingredients to within 2.5 cm/1 in of the edges. Brush the edges of the dough with water and fold over the filling to give the traditional pasty shape. Press the edges firmly together to seal and transfer the pasties on to the baking sheet. To make the glaze, whisk together the egg and milk and brush over each pasty. Bake in a preheated oven at 220°C/425°F/gas mark 7 for 15 minutes then reduce the oven temperature to 180°C/350°F/gas mark 4 for a further 25–30 minutes to bake the pasties until crisp and golden brown.

the home of cheddar

With such a perfect grazing environment for cattle, West Country milk is famously high in butterfat making it excellent for superior cream, cheese and butter. It's no wonder that clotted cream comes from this region! But more famous still is West Country cheese. It would be easy to write a whole chapter of bread recipes using cheeses from this region but, in the name of balance and in order not to show regional bias, I've focused on the most famous and the most widely made cheese in the world – Cheddar – which originates from my home county of Somerset.

It is said that this cheese was first discovered when a milkmaid accidentally left a pail of milk, for safety, in the Cheddar Gorge caves. When the maid returned to recover this milk she found that it had transformed into a tasty new substance and Cheddar cheese was born.

Originally the cheese had to be produced within thirty miles of Wells Cathedral to be called Cheddar, but as its popularity grew, in the 18th century more stringent requirements were enforced to preserve the original character of the local cheese.

King Henry II declared Cheddar cheese the best in Britain. Producers attribute the distinct Cheddar flavour to the rich pastures of Somerset and the ideal storage conditions available.

cheddar cheese and apple loaf

you need

2 large eggs, beaten
3 tbsp melted butter
100 g/3½ oz/1 cup grated Cox's apple
½ tsp salt
75 g/3 oz/1 cup grated mature Cheddar cheese
375 g/13 oz/2½ cups plain flour
1 tbsp baking powder
1 tbsp porridge oats

to make

Pour the eggs and butter into the breadmaker bucket followed by the apple, salt, cheese, flour and baking powder. Fit the bucket into the breadmaker and set to the cake or scone programme. If you have an adjustable crust facility on your machine, select the dark setting. After a few minutes of the mixing cycle, scrape down the mixture on the sides of the bucket with a plastic spatula to ensure all the ingredients are evenly mixed. When the mixing part of the cycle is complete, sprinkle the mixture with the porridge oats. Once cooked, carefully shake the cake from the bucket and stand it the right way up on a wire cooling rack. Leave to cool.

cheddar cheese and walnut bread

In this tasty bread traditional Cheddar cheese is combined with another classic West country ingredient – walnuts. Introduced to Britain by the Romans, it's no surprise that the common walnut tree *Juglans regia* was historically grown in the Vale of Pewsey and Bath.

you need

275 ml/10 fl oz/1¼ cups water
2 tbsp walnut oil
½ tsp paprika powder
1½ tsp mustard powder
1 tsp mixed dried herbs
1½ tsp salt
2 tbsp granulated sugar
75 g/3 oz/1 cup grated strong Cheddar cheese
225 g/8 oz/1½ cups strong wholemeal flour
225 g/8 oz/1½ cups very strong white bread flour
1½ tsp instant or fast-acting dried yeast
100 g/3½ oz/⅞ cup walnut pieces

to make

Pour the water and oil into the breadmaker bucket, followed by the spices, herbs, salt and sugar. Cover with the flour and sprinkle the yeast over the top. Fit the bucket into the breadmaker and set to the basic white programme. Add the walnuts according to your manual's instructions, usually at the beginning of the second kneading cycle or when the machine bleeps. Once cooked, carefully shake the loaf from the bucket and stand it the right way up on a wire cooling rack. Leave the bread to cool for at least an hour before slicing and/or removing the paddle if necessary.

variation: This loaf is also delicious made using Dorset Blue Vinney Cheese in place of the Cheddar.

devon pot cake

This Devon cake is so called because it was traditionally cooked in a pot on the range. If you prefer, the dried fruit can be substituted for blackberries, blackcurrants, apples or gooseberries as traditionally it was made with whatever fruit was plentiful at the time. If you are using fresh fruit, use the same weight as given below for the currants. Use either whole fresh berries or peeled, chopped apples and pears.

you need

300 ml/11 fl oz/1 3/8 cups full cream milk
1 large egg, beaten
pinch of salt
100 g/3 1/2 oz/7/16 cup very soft butter
50 g/2 oz/1/4 cup hard white vegetable fat, at room temperature
100 g/3 1/2 oz/5/8 cup currants
375 g/13 oz/2 1/2 cups self-raising flour

to make

Pour the milk into the breadmaker bucket followed by the egg, salt, butter, fat and currants. Cover with the flour and fit the bucket into the breadmaker. Set to the cake programme. Once cooked, remove the bucket from the machine and leave the cake to cool for 5 minutes. Carefully shake the loaf from the bucket and stand it the right way up on a wire cooling rack.

cheltenham cakes

Cheltenham Cakes are traditionally served warm with butter.

Makes 10

you need

50 ml/2 fl oz/¼ cup melted butter

275 ml/10 fl oz/1¼ cups full cream milk

2 tsp granulated sugar

450 g/16 oz/3 cups strong white bread flour

2 tsp instant or fast-acting dried yeast

to make

Lightly grease a baking tray. Pour the butter and milk into the breadmaker bucket and add the sugar. Cover the wet ingredients with the flour and sprinkle the yeast over the top. Fit the bucket into the breadmaker and set to the dough programme. When the cycle is complete, turn the dough out on to a lightly floured surface and knead until smooth. Divide the dough into 10 equally sized pieces and shape each piece into a flat cake. Put the cakes on to the baking sheet and bake in a preheated oven at 200°C/400°F/gas mark 6 for 15–20 minutes until golden.

south east

south east

Bordered by Bedford in the north and the Channel Islands in the south, this corner of Britain encompasses our capital city and major centres for both industry and tourism, including Oxford and Canterbury. Kent, known as the Garden of England, boasts a landscape punctuated with apple, pear and cherry orchards together with the hop gardens that have produced the essential flavour ingredients for its beer since the 17th century. In a region renowned for fruit production, it is fitting that it was here that our most famous apple varieties, Cox's Orange Pippin and Bramley, were originally propagated.

The fertile soils of the south coast and the inland counties provide food and fodder for cattle and sheep, and the perfect environment for the production of the cereal crops wheat, barley and oats, while the pure waters of Hampshire grow some of our finest watercress. Around London itself, although regional food is less apparent, specialities like Chelsea Buns (page 50) can be found. In Oxfordshire Mrs Sarah Jane Cooper first made Oxford Marmalade in 1874, while in neighbouring Banbury, the town's famous Banbury Cakes (opposite) are produced in the place where the nursery rhyme 'Ride a Cock Horse' originates.

While London itself does not produce a significant amount of food in an agricultural sense, its role as our capital and home of the famous markets of Billingsgate (the UK's largest inland fish market), Smithfield (where livestock and meat have been traded since the 10th century) and Nine Elms (the successor to the famous Covent Garden Market, selling fruit, vegetables and flowers) gives it a unique role in our food distribution. Today farmers' markets have also reached the capital and with London's popular Borough Market hosting a gourmet retail event every weekend, regional specialities from all over Britain are easily available here. This, together with London's large and varied population, means our capital is home to a host of native specialities while offering authentic cuisines from the rest of the world.

banbury cake

The nursery rhyme 'Ride a Cock Horse' put the town of Banbury firmly on the British map. The fact that it has been suggested that the 'fine lady' could have been either Lady Godiva or Elizabeth I gives us some indication of when this famous rhyme was first coined. Banbury is also famous for its cakes which, as this early 18th-century recipe shows, were traditionally yeast-leavened, unlike the pastry-based Banbury cakes that are still sold today.

This cake is a lovely example of the way in which spices can add extra magic to your loaves. As the port of London started to receive spices from all over the world, and these spices made their way across the region, bakers and housewives started to experiment. The combination of spices in this cake creates the very distinct taste of Banbury Cake.

you need

250 ml/9 fl oz/1⅛ cups milk
2 tsp rose water
75 g/3 oz/⅝ cup very soft butter
1 tbsp sugar
1 tsp salt
½ tsp ground mace
½ tsp ground cloves
3 tsp caraway seeds
225 g/8 oz/1½ cups very strong white bread flour
225 g/8 oz/1½ cups plain flour
1½ tsp instant or fast-acting dried yeast
100 g/3½ oz/⅝ cup currants

to make

Pour the milk into the breadmaker bucket, followed by the rose water and butter. Add the sugar, salt, spices and caraway seeds. Cover the ingredients with the flour and finally sprinkle the yeast over the top. Fit the bucket into the breadmaker and set to the basic white programme. Add the currants according to your manual's instructions, usually at the beginning of the second kneading cycle or when the machine bleeps. Once cooked, carefully shake the loaf from the bucket and stand it the right way up on a wire cooling rack. Leave the bread to cool for at least an hour before slicing and/or removing the paddle if necessary.

simnel yeast cake

Simnel Cake is often associated with Mothering Sunday. The reasons for this link vary. Some connect it with the Roman custom of honouring the goddess of motherhood in spring when the Romans made small cakes of a special flour called *simila* (from which the word simnel comes) to offer at her shrine. Others link it to the custom that pressured employers to let young people working far from home return to their mothers at least once a year, taking with them a basket of goodies which would include a simnel cake. Below is a traditional yeast-based recipe.

you need

200 ml/7 fl oz/$\frac{7}{8}$ cup full cream milk
3 medium eggs, beaten
125 g/4 oz/$\frac{1}{2}$ cup very soft butter
50 g/2 oz/$\frac{5}{16}$ cup soft light brown sugar
1 tsp salt
1 tsp mixed spice
225 g/8 oz/$1\frac{1}{2}$ cups very strong white bread flour
225 g/8 oz/$1\frac{1}{2}$ cups plain flour
$2\frac{1}{2}$ tsp instant or fast-acting dried yeast
1 tbsp chopped preserved ginger, drained
50 g/2 oz/$\frac{1}{4}$ cup chopped mixed peel
100 g/$3\frac{1}{2}$ oz/$\frac{3}{4}$ cup currants
1 x 450g/16 oz block marzipan

For the glaze:
2 tbsp full cream milk

to make

Lightly grease a 20 cm/8 in loose-bottomed cake tin with butter. Pour the milk and eggs into the breadmaker bucket, followed by the butter, sugar, salt and spices. Cover the mixture with the flour and sprinkle the yeast over the top. Fit the bucket into the breadmaker and set to the dough programme. Add the currants according to your manufacturer's instructions, usually at the beginning of the second kneading cycle or when the machine bleeps. When the cycle is complete, turn the dough out on to a floured surface and carefully knead until smooth. This is very light dough and can be quite sticky to handle. I find a floured scraper or plastic spatula invaluable to help turn and knead it. Divide the dough into two equally-sized pieces and shape each into a circle. Lightly press one of the pieces of dough into the bottom of the cake tin. Mould the marzipan in your hands to soften it and then roll it out to fit the dimensions of the tin. You may find it helpful to place the tin on top of the marzipan and cut around the edge to get a good fit. Place the marzipan on top of the dough in the cake tin. Then cover this with the second piece of dough and lightly press it out to cover the marzipan. Cover the cake with a tea towel and leave in a warm place to prove until well risen. Brush the top layer with milk and bake in a preheated oven at 200°C/400°F/gas mark 6 for 30 minutes until risen and golden. Leave the cake to cool in the tin for 5–10 minutes to help prevent the layers from separating as you remove the cake from the tin. Loosen the cake from the edge of the tin with a plastic spatula and transfer to a wire rack to cool.

hops

The Latin for hop is *Humulus lupulus*, or wolf of the woods, and the plant is distantly related to hemp, nettle and elm. When these tall climbing plants flower in July the female flowers bear the cones – which are the essential ingredient for the brewing process.

Hop cones and oast houses are regular features of the Kent countryside and are testament to the times when families from London's East End used to make an annual holiday of hop picking. While in the 17th century conditions for these workers were extremely poor, in later times families would regard the picking season and its rural freedom a pleasing change from their cramped urban existence. Curiously, hops were originally grown as a vegetable and it wasn't until the 16th century that they were used in brewing. Fires inside oast houses were used to dry the hops before they were sent all over the country as the essential ingredients for the beer industry.

rustic beer bread

No chapter on the South East of Britain would be complete without tribute to the brewing industry and this rustic beer bread encompasses all the flavour of traditional real ale. Kent hosts a thriving beer festival every year to showcase its beer and ale, with events taking place in Maidstone and Gravesend. I've tried this recipe with many different beers and each changes the flavour very slightly. So why not give it a go with your favourite real ale?

you need

250 ml/9 fl oz/1⅛ cups beer, warmed
3 tbsp sunflower oil
2 tbsp malt extract
1½ tsp salt
70 g/2½ oz/½ cup strong wholemeal flour
70 g/2½ oz/½ cup soft grain white bread flour
150 g/5¼ oz/1 cup country grain strong brown bread flour
150 g/5¼ oz/1 cup very strong white bread flour
2 tsp instant or fast-acting dried yeast

to make

Pour the beer into the breadmaker bucket, followed by the oil, malt extract and salt. Cover the mixture with the flour and finally sprinkle the yeast over the top. Fit the bucket into the breadmaker and set to the basic white programme. Once cooked, carefully shake the loaf out of the bucket and stand it the right way up on a wire cooling rack. Leave the bread to cool for at least an hour before slicing and/or removing the paddle if necessary.

oast cakes

Oasts are the distinctive brick buildings found in Kent where hops are dried. The hops were spread on wooden floors of the buildings to dry by the heat of the fires below. The hot air and steam from the process escaped through the distinctive cowl at the top of the oast. Drying was an extremely skilled and prestigious job and men doing this would stay in the oast houses until the harvest was complete.

By contrast conditions for hop pickers (especially in the 17th century) were extremely poor and this recipe is testament to how they lived. Oast cakes were made by hop pickers, who would mix up the dough early in the morning, leave it to rest all day and then fry the cakes over a campfire at their afternoon break. Originally Oast Cakes would have been shaped into balls and shallow fried in lard, but I find deep-frying in oil a healthier and more convenient alternative.

These cakes are like little fried dumplings and are made using ingredients that were easy for the pickers to come by. The beer gives them a distinctive yeasty character, with the sweetness from the sugar and fruit traditionally providing the energy and sustenance needed to complete the hard day's work.

Makes 16

you need

75 ml/3 fl oz/$\frac{3}{8}$ cup melted butter

8 tbsp beer

4 tbsp water

2 tsp granulated sugar

$\frac{1}{2}$ tsp salt

375 g/13 oz/$2\frac{1}{2}$ cups plain flour

2 tsp instant or fast-acting dried yeast

100g/$3\frac{1}{2}$ oz/$\frac{5}{8}$ cup currants

For the finish:

vegetable oil for deep frying

caster sugar

to make

Pour the butter, beer and water into the breadmaker bucket. Add the sugar, salt and flour and sprinkle the yeast over the top. Fit the bucket into the breadmaker and set to the dough programme. Add the currants according to your manual's instructions, usually at the beginning of the second kneading cycle or when the machine bleeps. When the cycle is complete, turn the dough out on to a lightly floured surface and knead until smooth. Divide the dough into 16 equally-sized pieces and shape each piece into a smooth round about the size of a golf ball. Pre-heat the deep fat fryer or half fill a wok with vegetable oil and heat until very hot. Deep-fry the cakes, very carefully and a few at a time, for 3–4 minutes until nicely browned. Remove the cakes from the oil, drain on kitchen paper and quickly roll them in caster sugar. Serve immediately.

from the garden of england

The warm, moist climate and rich soil make the Kent Weald an exceptionally fertile region. Situated in the triangle of land bordered by Cranbrook (known as the capital of the Weald), Maidstone and Royal Tunbridge Wells, the Weald boasts rolling countryside, native woodlands, orchards and hop fields. Both fruit and vegetables have thrived in Kent since Roman times; in fact, it was the Romans who first introduced cherries to the shores of Kent. Coming into season in June, English cherries are still available from local growers and are often sold at the farm gate.

kentish huffkins

Traditionally made by Kentish maids, Huffkins are oval flat loaves with a soft crust and a deep indentation in the centre. They have an open texture and can be enjoyed sliced and buttered, though for a traditional Kentish touch, the hole in the middle can be filled with hot cherries – a thrifty way of using the glut of fruit from the cherry harvest – and the dish served as a dessert.

Makes 8–10

you need

150 ml/5 fl oz/5/8 cup water

125 ml/4 fl oz/1/2 cup semi-skimmed milk

1 tsp salt

1 tbsp granulated sugar

150 g/5 1/4 oz/1 cup plain flour

300 g/11 oz/2 cups strong white bread flour

2 1/2 tsp instant or fast-acting dried yeast

to make

Lightly grease a baking tray. Pour the water and milk into the breadmaker bucket, followed by the salt and sugar. Cover the ingredients with the two flours and finally sprinkle the yeast over the top. Fit the bucket into the breadmaker and set to the dough programme. When the cycle is complete, turn the dough out on to a lightly floured surface and knead until smooth. Divide the dough into 8–10 equally-sized pieces and roll each piece into an oval cake about 1 cm/1/2 in thick. Put the cakes on to the baking sheet, cover with a tea towel and leave in a warm place to prove until doubled in size. Just before baking, make a deep indentation in the top of each cake with your thumb. Bake in a preheated oven at 220°C/425°F/gas mark 7 for 15 minutes until golden brown. Once cooked, stand them the right way up on a wire cooling rack and leave to cool.

london's pride

London has always been big for food tradition – whether it's the Eel, Pie and Mash Houses that have existed since the 18th century or the barrows found on street corners selling winkles, prawns, cockles and mussels. Dishes like boiled beef and carrots, bubble and squeak and roast chestnuts sold from carts on the street are all synonymous with our capital, as are a host of baked specialities based on bread dough.

london buns

These are delicious currant finger buns, covered in a sweet sugar icing.

Makes 8–10

you need

375 g/13 oz/$2\frac{1}{2}$ cups very strong white bread flour
70 g/$2\frac{1}{2}$ oz/$\frac{1}{2}$ cup plain flour
75 g/3 oz/$\frac{5}{16}$ cup hard white vegetable fat
200 ml/7 fl oz/$\frac{7}{8}$ cup water
75 ml/3 fl oz/$\frac{3}{8}$ cup full cream milk
3 tbsp granulated sugar
1 tsp salt
$\frac{1}{2}$ tsp ground nutmeg
$2\frac{1}{2}$ tsp instant or fast-acting dried yeast
50 g/2 oz/$\frac{5}{16}$ cup currants
3 tsp caraway seeds (optional)

For the icing:

150 g/$5\frac{1}{4}$ oz/$1\frac{1}{8}$ cups icing sugar
$1\frac{1}{2}$ tbsp warm water

to make

Lightly grease a baking tray. Put the two flours into a bowl and rub in the fat until the mixture resembles breadcrumbs. Pour the water and milk into the breadmaker bucket and add the sugar, salt and nutmeg. Cover the liquid with the flour mixture and finally sprinkle the yeast over the top. Fit the bucket into the breadmaker and set to the dough programme. Add the currants (and caraway seeds if using) according to your manual's instructions, usually at the beginning of the second kneading cycle or when the machine bleeps. When the cycle is complete, turn the dough out on to a lightly floured surface and knead until smooth. Divide the dough into 8–10 equally sized pieces and shape each piece into a finger roll. Place the buns on to the baking sheet, cover with a tea towel and leave in a warm place to prove until doubled in size. Bake in a preheated oven at 200°C/400°F/gas mark 6 for 12–15 minutes until golden. Transfer them to a wire cooling rack and leave to cool completely. To make the icing, blend the sugar and water together until smooth and spread over the top of each bun.

st clements buns

'Oranges and Lemons say the bells of St Clements.' In celebration of this old nursery rhyme centred on London's famous bells, I've devised this delicious recipe for rich buns flavoured with citrus and spice. Adding grated citrus peel to bread is an excellent way of introducing both flavour and aroma. Whether you pare the rind or finely grate it is up to you, but whichever you choose, make sure you don't include the bitter white pith or the flavour will be spoiled. The flavour of these buns is enhanced further with spices; the freshness of cardamom and distinctive sweet, nutty flavour of cinnamon.

Makes 14

you need

200 ml/7 fl oz/7/8 cup semi-skimmed milk
2 medium eggs, beaten
100 ml/3½ fl oz/7/16 cup melted butter
zest of 1 lemon
zest of 1 orange
½ tsp ground cardamom
½ tsp ground cinnamon
100 g/3½ oz/7/16 cup caster sugar
1½ tsp salt
450 g/16 oz/3 cups very strong white bread flour
2½ tsp instant or fast-acting dried yeast

For the glaze:

1 egg
1 tbsp water
pinch of salt
2 tbsp marmalade, sieved to remove the rind

to make

Lightly grease a baking tray. Pour the milk, eggs and butter into the breadmaker bucket and add the rind, spices, sugar and salt. Cover the mixture with the flour and sprinkle the yeast over the top. Fit the bucket into the breadmaker and set to the dough programme. When the cycle is complete, turn the dough out on to a lightly floured surface and knead until smooth. Divide the dough into 14 equally sized pieces and shape each piece into a round roll. Put the rolls onto the baking sheet and cut a cross in the top of each with a sharp knife. Cover with a tea towel and leave in a warm place to prove until doubled in size. Bake in a preheated oven at 200°C/400°F/gas mark 6 for 12–15 minutes until golden. Brush with marmalade while still warm.

chelsea buns

Chelsea Buns are a London delicacy and one of the most famous of all our traditional breads. Originally the sweet, fruit-laden buns were sold by 'Captain Bun' from the Old Chelsea Bun House in Pimlico where King George III was said to be a regular customer. Sadly, these premises were destroyed in 1839 but the recipe lives on today and Chelsea Buns can now be found in bakeries nationwide.

Makes 12

you need

200 ml/7 fl oz/$^{7}/_{8}$ cup full cream milk

75 ml/3 fl oz/$^{3}/_{8}$ cup melted butter

2 medium eggs, beaten

2 tsp sugar

1 tsp salt

450 g/16 oz/3 cups very strong white bread flour

2 tsp instant or fast-acting dried yeast

For the filling:

100 g/3$^{1}/_{2}$ oz/$^{3}/_{4}$ cup mixed dried fruit

50 g/2 oz/$^{5}/_{16}$ cup light soft brown sugar

2 tbsp melted butter

For the glaze:

runny honey

to make

Lightly grease a 30 cm/12 in square baking tray. To make the buns, pour the milk, butter and eggs into the breadmaker bucket. Add the sugar, salt and flour and then sprinkle the yeast over the top. Fit the bucket into the breadmaker and set to the dough programme. When the cycle is complete, turn the dough out on to a lightly floured surface and knead until smooth. Roll the dough out into a large rectangle. To make the filling, mix the dried fruit with the sugar. Brush the dough with the melted butter and, leaving a 2.5cm/1 in border around the edges, sprinkle the fruit mixture over. Roll the dough up like a Swiss roll, starting at the long end. Press the edges together to seal. Cut the roll into 12 equally sized slices and place, cut-side up, onto the baking tray. Arrange the buns so that they will touch one another once they have proved. Cover with a tea towel and leave in a warm place to prove until doubled in size. Bake in a preheated oven at 190°C/375°F/gas mark 5 for 15–20 minutes until well risen and golden. Brush the buns with the honey while still hot and leave them to cool slightly in the tray before transferring them to a wire rack to cool fully.

canterbury pudding

This delicious pudding has a cake-like texture and is scented with lemon and brandy. It is fantastic served fresh from your breadmaker with thick cream or custard.

you need

6 tbsp brandy

2 large eggs, beaten

150 ml/5 fl oz/$\frac{5}{8}$ cup melted butter

zest and juice of 2 lemons

100 g/$3\frac{1}{2}$ oz/$\frac{7}{16}$ cup caster sugar

150 g/$5\frac{1}{4}$ oz/$2\frac{1}{2}$ cups fresh white breadcrumbs

150 g/$5\frac{1}{4}$ oz/1 cup self-raising flour

1 tsp baking powder

to make

Pour the brandy, eggs, butter, lemon rind and lemon juice into the breadmaker bucket. Add the sugar, breadcrumbs, flour and baking powder. Fit the bucket into the breadmaker and set to the cake programme. After 5 minutes of the mixing cycle, scrape down the sides of the bucket with a plastic spatula to ensure all the ingredients are evenly mixed. Once cooked, remove the bucket from the machine and leave to cool for 5 minutes before turning the pudding out on to a serving dish. Serve hot.

isle of wight doughnuts

Doughnuts have a historical link with the Isle of Wight – the island claims to be the first place in the UK that developed them. References to doughnuts can be found in local shroving customs and songs. Shroving was the local name given to Shrove Tuesday celebrations and it was said that shrovers would gather in the early morning and go from house to house singing for their shrove cakes (pancakes or doughnuts). By doing this the poor and the young were able to get their fill of rich goodies before Lent. Traditionally, in contrast to today's more common jam-filled varieties (see recipe on page 90), Isle of Wight Doughnuts were filled with plums or currants and candied peel as in the recipe below.

Makes 16

you need

225 g/8 oz/$1\frac{1}{2}$ cups strong white bread flour
225 g/8 oz/$1\frac{1}{2}$ cups plain flour
75 g/3 oz/$\frac{5}{8}$ cups butter
1 medium egg, beaten
225 ml/8 fl oz/1 cup full cream milk
$\frac{1}{4}$ tsp grated nutmeg
50 g/2 oz/$\frac{5}{16}$ cup caster sugar
$2\frac{1}{2}$ tsp instant or fast-acting dried yeast

For the filling:

50 g/2 oz/$\frac{1}{4}$ cup mixed peel
75 g/3 oz/$\frac{1}{2}$ cup currants

For the finish:

vegetable oil
caster sugar

to make

To make the doughnuts, put the flour into a large bowl and rub in the butter until the mixture resembles fine breadcrumbs. Pour the egg and milk into the breadmaker bucket, followed by the nutmeg and sugar. Cover the liquid with the flour mixture and sprinkle the yeast over the top. Fit the bucket into the breadmaker and set to the dough programme. To make the filling, mix the peel and currants together and set aside. When the cycle is complete, turn the dough out on to a lightly floured surface and knead until smooth. Divide the dough into 16 equally-sized pieces. Flatten each piece of dough and place a little of the filling mixture in the centre. Gather the edges together over the filling, seal and roll into a ball. Preheat the deep fat fryer or half fill a wok with vegetable oil and heat on the hob until hot. Fry the doughnuts in batches over a slow heat for about 15 minutes, until they are puffy and golden. Drain them on kitchen paper and roll in caster sugar. Serve warm.

tomato bread with watercress

In Hampshire in particular, the substrata of chalk makes a perfect filter for the pure water that is essential for the production of high-quality watercress. It's an unlikely ingredient for a loaf but provides the perfect peppery flavour to complement tomato and makes attractive green specks in this rich orange bread.

you need

225 ml/8 fl oz/1 cup water
3 tbsp sunflower oil
3 tbsp tomato purée
2 tbsp granulated sugar
1½ tsp salt
25 g/1 oz fresh watercress leaves
pinch of nutmeg
150 g/5¼ oz/1 cup strong brown flour
300 g/11 oz/2 cups strong white bread flour
1¼ tsp instant or fast-acting dried yeast

to make

Pour the water, oil, tomato purée, sugar and salt into the breadmaker bucket. Add the watercress leaves, nutmeg, flour and finally sprinkle the yeast over the top. Fit the bucket into the breadmaker and set to the basic white programme. Once cooked, carefully shake the loaf from the bucket and stand it the right way up on a wire cooling rack. Leave the bread to cool for at least an hour before slicing and/or removing the paddle if necessary.

eastern counties

eastern counties

The counties of Norfolk, Suffolk, Essex, Cambridgeshire and Lincolnshire form the easterly edge of Britain and offer some of our best regional specialities. Take the small but succulent Cromer Crab for instance: the little crabs caught by fishermen from this small town on the north coast of Norfolk are too small to fetch good prices at Billingsgate, so almost the entire catch is sold locally from the windows of road side houses. Freshly cooked they are perfect when accompanied by good, homemade bread.

The countryside here is as varied as it comes – the fens and the broads lie flat as far as the eye can see and offer the perfect contrast to the rounder landscapes of Suffolk and Essex. With this diversity of landscape comes very different environments: windmills are evidence of windy weather, while the relatively dry climate and fertile soils make this region the provider of many of our vegetable staples.

The Eastern Counties enjoy good agricultural conditions and the bounty of the coastline. The sea brings cockles, whitebait and oysters and the fields of East Anglia grow wheat, oats and barley, with mustard also being produced from seed grown in the brilliant yellow fields around Norwich. Soft fruit, too, is grown in profusion, especially around the areas of Wisbech in Norfolk and Tiptree in Essex. With an abundance of gooseberries, redcurrants, strawberries, blackcurrants, raspberries, blackberries, cherries and plums, it's no surprise that jam making is also big business here.

Lincolnshire is known as the maritime county of England. Gastronomically, it is famed for its pork products (including sausages and stuffed chine) and for its plum bread (see opposite for my recipe). It is also a major vegetable producer for the rest of the country. Neighbouring Cambridgeshire is home to the village of Stilton – the famous cheese is named after this village, even though it was never made there.

lincolnshire plum bread

Just as with plum pudding, the plums in this famous bread are generally dried fruits like currants, raisins and sultanas. In fact, it appears to be something of a joke in Lincolnshire that its plum bread never contained plums! The reason for this remains a mystery as even the web sites of many local producers ask readers for suggestions as to why this is the case! Several variations of this recipe exist, but all comprise a rich bread heavily laden with fruit and spice. The variation I've chosen uses succulent prunes in addition to the more usual dried fruits and is flavoured with allspice – the only spice (apart from chilli) native to the Western hemisphere. Columbus considered allspice to be a mix of cloves, cinnamon and nutmeg and today it is a popular choice for flavouring both sweet and savoury dishes.

you need

2 large eggs, beaten
100 ml/3½ fl oz/7/16 cup melted butter
125 ml/4 fl oz/½ cup milk
1 tsp ground cinnamon
1 tsp ground allspice
4 tbsp granulated sugar
1 tsp salt
450 g/16 oz/3 cups strong white bread flour
1½ tsp instant or fast-acting dried yeast
75 g/3 oz/⅜ cup roughly chopped ready to eat dried plums (prunes)
25 g/1 oz/⅛ cup currants
25 g/1 oz/⅛ cup sultanas

For the glaze:
1 egg
1 tbsp water
pinch of salt

to make

Pour the egg, butter and milk into the breadmaker bucket, followed by the spices, sugar and salt. Cover the mixture with the flour and sprinkle the yeast over the top. Fit the bucket into the breadmaker and set to the basic white programme. Add the plums, currants and sultanas according to the manual's instructions, usually at the beginning or middle of the second kneading cycle or when the machine bleeps. Forty-five minutes before the end of the cycle, whisk together the egg, water and salt to make the glaze. Carefully lift the lid of the machine and brush on the egg wash. When cooked, carefully shake the loaf from the bucket and stand it the right way up on a wire cooling rack. Leave for at least an hour before slicing and/or removing the paddle if necessary.

marlborough's ipswich almond pudding

If you've ever struggled when making you own egg custard then this wonderfully light pudding, made quickly and easily in your breadmaker, will be a dream come true. The breadmaker takes away all the usual difficulties of cooking egg custard – there's no need for a bain marie, or wondering if it's quite set – just pop the ingredients into your machine and press 'start'. It couldn't be easier. This traditional 18th-century recipe is delicious served with a selection of soft summer fruits either fresh or lightly poached in a sugar syrup (see below).

you need

450 ml/16 fl oz/2 cups full cream milk
150 ml/5 fl oz/$\frac{5}{8}$ cup double cream
3 large eggs, beaten
50 g/2 oz/$\frac{3}{4}$ cup fresh white breadcrumbs
50g/2 oz/$\frac{3}{16}$ cup granulated sugar
175g/6 oz/1$\frac{3}{4}$ cups ground almonds
25g/1 oz/$\frac{1}{8}$ cup butter

to make

Pour the milk, cream and eggs into the breadmaker bucket. Cover the mixture with the breadcrumbs, sugar and almonds. Cut the butter into small pieces and add to the mixture. Fit the bucket into the breadmaker and set to the cake programme. After 5 minutes of the mixing cycle, scrape down the mixture on the sides of the bucket with a plastic spatula to ensure all the ingredients are evenly combined. When cooked, remove the bucket from the machine and leave the pudding to cool for 5 minutes before turning out onto a plate. This pudding is delicious served lukewarm with fresh or poached fruit.

the best poached fruit

Poached fruit – fruit compote or stewed fruit – is one of the simplest yet most effective ways of preparing our native fruits. Versatile and tasty, these compotes can be served as an accompaniment to desserts like the one above, or simply with yogurt, cream or an egg custard. Choose fruit that is juicy but not over-ripe. Pears, plums, apples, cherries and all our British berries are perfect. Peel, core and stone the fruit as necessary. Cut into pieces if you wish.

Make a sugar syrup by putting 300 ml/11 fl oz/1$\frac{3}{8}$ cups water and 225g/8 oz/1 cup of sugar into a saucepan. (For variety you could add spices such as vanilla, cinnamon or cloves to the syrup, or substitute brandy or wine for a couple of tablespoons of the water.) Bring the mixture to the boil and simmer for a few minutes until the sugar has dissolved completely and the liquid is slightly thickened. Add your chosen fruit and cook gently until the fruit is just soft enough to be cut with a spoon, but not enough to fall apart. Serve hot, warm, or cold.

beer, barley and cyder too

Grain production is big business in the east and out of this comes a thriving beer-making industry spanning most counties in the region. With many award-winning beers, including Crouch Vale Brewer's Gold from Essex, Suffolk's Green King IPA, Milton Electra from Cambridgeshire and Spectrum Old Stoatwobbler from Norfolk, there's something for every taste; and, with local cyder (spelled with a 'y') also a favourite tipple, it's obvious that apple production is prevalent here, too.

With the region's relatively long, sunny summers and low rainfall, the area also has some excellent vineyards producing arguably some of our best native wine. Chilford Hall Vineyard at Linton in Cambridgeshire, for example, grows early-cropping vines like Muller-Thurgau, Ortega, Huxelrebe, Schonenburger and Siegerrebe to produce a range of dry and medium dry white wines, pink wine and even sparkling pink wines.

barley bread

Bread made using solely barley flour is not possible in a breadmaker and, even if made by hand, it has what I think is an acquired taste and texture. When mixed in small quantities with good strong white flour, however, the loaf transforms into something really special – a smooth, even-textured bread that is greyish-white in colour and has a wholesome, yet delicate taste. This is a versatile bread that's perfect for daily use – for everything from toast to sandwiches.

you need

250 ml/9 fl oz/$1\frac{1}{8}$ cups water
3 tbsp buttermilk
1 tsp salt
1 tbsp granulated sugar
100 g/$3\frac{1}{2}$ oz/$\frac{3}{4}$ cup barley flour
350 g/12 oz/$2\frac{1}{4}$ cups very strong white bread flour
$1\frac{1}{2}$ tsp instant or fast-acting dried yeast

to make

Pour the water and buttermilk into the breadmaker, followed by the salt and sugar. Cover the liquid with the flour and sprinkle the yeast over the top. Fit the bucket into the breadmaker and set to the basic white programme. When cooked, carefully shake the loaf from the bucket and stand it the right way up on a wire cooling rack. Leave for at least an hour before slicing and/or removing the paddle if necessary.

malt loaf

Malt extract – the concentrated infusion of germinated barley – is the essential ingredient for malt loaf. It can be found in jars at most health food shops. Malt Loaf is a British classic and something that I think breadmakers make really well. Light and airy, this bread is perfect simply served with butter. Trust me – make it and it'll disappear in a flash!

you need

250 ml/9 fl oz/1⅛ cups water
1 tbsp sunflower oil
3 tbsp malt extract
1 tsp salt
2 tbsp dark muscovado sugar
450 g/16 oz/3 cups very strong white bread flour
1¼ tsp instant or fast-acting dried yeast
50 g/2 oz/¼ cup sultanas

to make

Pour the water and oil into the breadmaker, followed by the malt extract, salt and sugar. Add the flour and then sprinkle the yeast over the top. Fit the bucket into the breadmaker and set to the basic white programme. Add the sultanas according to your manual's instructions, usually at the beginning of the second kneading cycle or when the machine bleeps. Once cooked, carefully shake the loaf from the bucket and stand it the right way up on a wire cooling rack. Leave to cool for at least an hour before slicing and/or removing the paddle if necessary.

spiced pumpkin bread

We don't think of pumpkin when considering British food: it's usually associated with American specialities like Pumpkin Pie. However, during my research for this book I found several mentions of pumpkin bread in British recipes made as early as the 1750s, when it was used to improve the keeping qualities of bread and as a bulking agent to make dough go further. The pumpkin in my Pumpkin Bread provides rich colour, a slightly sweet taste and a wonderful moistness to the loaf, making it perfect either served freshly sliced or toasted with butter, jam or honey. I attribute this loaf to the East simply because of a journey made last October to visit a friend in Norfolk. On this journey I saw so many pumpkins for sale at farm gates and roadside stalls that I have since always thought of Norfolk as the pumpkin county of Britain.

you need

50 ml/2 fl oz/¼ cup semi-skimmed milk

225 g/8 oz/1 cup pumpkin purée (tinned, or see method below for instructions)

2 tsp runny honey

1¼ tsp salt

2 tbsp soft butter

1 tsp ground cinnamon

1 tsp ground ginger

450 g/16 oz/3 cups very strong white bread flour

1¼tsp instant or fast-acting dried yeast

For the glaze/top:

1 tbsp semi-skimmed milk

1 tbsp pumpkin seeds

to make

To make pumpkin purée, peel and deseed a pumpkin or squash and cut the flesh into cubes of about 2.5 cm/1 in. Put the pumpkin into a saucepan and add just enough boiling water to cover. Bring to the boil and simmer for 15–20 minutes until soft. Strain off the water and leave the pumpkin to cool slightly. Transfer the pumpkin to the food processor and blend until smooth.

Pour the milk into the breadmaker bucket, followed by the pumpkin purée and honey. Add the salt, sugar and spices. Cover the mixture with the flour and sprinkle the yeast over the top. Fit the bucket into the breadmaker and set to the basic white programme. 45 minutes before the end of the cycle, carefully lift the lid and brush the loaf with milk and sprinkle the pumpkin seeds over the top. When cooked, carefully shake the loaf from the bucket and stand it the right way up on a wire cooling rack. Leave for at least an hour before slicing and/or removing the paddle if necessary.

18th-century coconut bread

As with Spiced Pumpkin Bread (page 64), I was surprised to find coconut featuring in old English bread recipes. Obviously in the original version creamed or desiccated coconut was not used but instead long, detailed instructions were given on how to make the most of every part of this exotic nut. The recipes described how to grate the white flesh and brown rind and to use them to make a rich milk that would flavour the dough. Today with modern coconut products readily available, I've devised a 21st-century version of the original recipe which gives a delicately flavoured, moist loaf, speckled with tiny coconut pieces.

you need

125 ml/4 fl oz/½ cup water
175 ml/6 fl oz/¾ cup creamed coconut
50 g/2 oz/½ cup desiccated coconut
1 tbsp sugar
1 tsp salt
225 g/8 oz/1½ cups very strong white bread flour
225 g/8 oz/1½ cups wholesome white very strong bread flour
1½ tsp instant or fast-acting dried yeast

to make

Pour the water and creamed coconut into the breadmaker bucket. Add the desiccated coconut, sugar and salt. Cover the mixture with the flour and finally sprinkle the yeast over the top. Fit the bucket into the breadmaker and set to the basic white programme. Once cooked, carefully shake the loaf from the bucket and stand it the right way up on a wire cooling rack. Leave to cool for at least an hour before slicing and/or removing the paddle if necessary.

norfolk dumplings

The coastal marshes, fields of grain and flat fens of East Anglia provide shelter and the perfect breeding ground for partridge, pheasant, wild duck and woodcock, in addition to rabbit and hare. Many local dishes feature this game and the famous Norfolk Dumplings, made in the traditional way with yeast, rather than a chemical raising agent and suet. These dumplings look very similar to our modern variations, but as they are made with yeast and strong flour the taste and texture is far more closely related to bread than to a suet dough, making them, for me, a much more pleasing alternative. As with all dumplings, the flavour is drawn from the cooking liquor so I'd recommend cooking these in a hearty stew or casserole.

Makes 10

you need

225 ml/8 fl oz/1 cup water

1 tsp salt

1 tsp granulated sugar

450g/10 oz/3 cups strong white bread flour

2½ tsp instant or fast-acting dried yeast

to make

Pour the water into the breadmaker bucket, followed by the salt and sugar. Cover the mixture with the flour and sprinkle the yeast over the top. Fit the bucket into the breadmaker and set to the dough programme. When the cycle is complete, turn the dough out on to a lightly floured surface and knead until smooth. Divide the dough into 10 equally-sized pieces and shape each piece into a ball. Transfer the dumplings to a baking sheet and leave in a warm place to prove until doubled in size. To cook the dumplings, simmer them in a shallow pan of stock for about 30 minutes, or in a casserole or stew for the same amount of time.

norfolk floaters

Traditionally, Norfolk Floaters were served before the meat course with treacle or sugar to take the edge off the appetite. They are firm cakes with a dense, bread-like texture and shiny, smooth exterior. They epitomize traditional working-class food as they were created with cheap ingredients, cooked simply and designed to provide a rich source of carbohydrate to help give the energy needed for the long working day.

Norfolk Floaters can be made with the same mixture as Norfolk Dumplings. Simply shape the dough into 10 and roll each into a flat cake about the same thickness as a crumpet. Cook for 25 minutes in boiling water.

suffolk apple fritters with saffron cream

Imagine a light, crisp and bubbly batter coating sweet, soft slices of apple. Then top it all with a spoon of heavenly golden-yellow saffron-flavoured cream – delicious. Yeast batter for the finest homemade fritters is simple to make with a breadmaker and once you've tried it I guarantee you'll be using it for other fruits like pears and pineapples. Choose sweet dessert apples like Cox or Jonagold for this recipe, as they soften but hold their shape well when cooked and give a wonderful sweet taste. These fritters are excellent served with cream scented with saffron – a spice that was once grown in large quantities in Suffolk.

Serves 8–10

you need

150 ml/5 fl oz/$\frac{5}{8}$ cup milk
75 ml/3 fl oz/$\frac{3}{8}$ cup buttermilk
1 large egg, beaten
$\frac{1}{2}$ tsp salt
$\frac{1}{2}$ tbsp sugar
125 g/4 oz/$\frac{7}{8}$ cup strong white bread flour
$1\frac{1}{2}$ tsp instant or fast-acting dried yeast
4 eating apples

For the finish:
2 tbsp plain flour
vegetable oil
caster sugar

For the saffron cream:
350 ml/12 fl oz/$1\frac{1}{2}$ cups double cream
1 tsp saffron strands
2 tbsp icing sugar

to make

To make the batter, pour the milk, buttermilk and eggs into the breadmaker bucket, followed by the salt and sugar. Cover the mixture with the flour and sprinkle the yeast over the top. Fit the bucket into the breadmaker and set to the dough programme.

In the meantime, make the saffron cream. Measure 75ml/3 fl oz/$\frac{3}{8}$ cup of the double cream into a saucepan and add the saffron. Heat the mixture slowly until it boils, stirring continuously. Remove from the heat and leave to stand for 30 minutes until richly yellow. Strain the mix through a fine sieve. Whip the remaining double cream until stiff and then whisk in the icing sugar. Fold the cooled saffron infusion into the whipped cream. This will turn the mixture a warm yellow colour. Once thoroughly mixed, cover the bowl with cling film and chill until required.

When the dough programme is complete, the batter should be thick and bubbly. Depending on your particular machine, you may need to leave the batter a little longer in a warm place to ferment, until it has risen at least half way up the bucket.

Peel and core the apples, then slice into rings and coat in the plain flour. Preheat the deep fat fryer or half fill a wok with vegetable oil and heat on the hob until very hot. Dip each fritter in the batter and immediately fry for 2–3 minutes until crisp and golden, in batches of two or three. Drain the fritters on kitchen paper, dust with caster sugar and serve immediately with the saffron cream.

stilton and walnut bread with port

Stilton is known as the 'King of Cheeses' and, although it's named after the Cambridgeshire village, it was never made there. Its origins lie in 18th-century trading when the town of Stilton was a trading post for coaches. Mr Cooper Thornhill, landlord of the Bell Inn at Stilton, introduced weary travellers to this curious blue-veined cheese. It is thought that he purchased it from a farmer's wife who made the cheese near Melton Mowbray where she lived.

The robust taste of our most popular blue cheese bursts through in this wholesome loaf. With English walnuts and cheese a classic combination, what better way to add texture to this truly excellent bread?

you need

225 ml/8 fl oz/1 cup water

4 tbsp port

2 tbsp sunflower oil

1 medium egg, beaten

1 tsp salt

1 tbsp granulated sugar

75 g/3 oz/¾ cup crumbled Stilton cheese

450 g/16 oz/3 cups wholesome white very strong bread flour

1½ tsp instant or fast-acting dried yeast

100 g/3½ oz/⅞ cup walnut pieces

to make

Pour the water, port, oil and egg into the breadmaker bucket, followed by the salt, sugar and cheese. Cover the mixture with the flour and sprinkle the yeast over the top. Fit the bucket into the breadmaker and set to the basic white programme. Add the walnuts according to your manual's instructions, usually at the beginning of the second kneading cycle or when the machine bleeps. Once cooked, carefully shake the loaf from the bucket and stand it the right way up on a wire cooling rack. Leave to cool.

british classics

Finally in this chapter I include two British classics – the Traditional Cottage Loaf and Muffins. I could have placed these recipes in many chapters in this book but felt they rested best here.

Largely because of its remoteness, I suppose, East Anglia has managed to retain many traditional village bakeries with the old-fashioned ovens that are synonymous with cottage loaves. English Muffins are placed here only because my memories of enjoying them are fixed to this area.

traditional cottage loaf

For me this is the quintessential British loaf as the shape reminds me so strongly of my childhood – I toasted slices of a cottage loaf on a fork in front of my grandparents' fire. If you've never eaten a cottage loaf you're in for a treat.Traditionally, these loaves were baked on the floor of a brick-built oven, giving conditions hard to replicate in the domestic kitchen. So, the method of baking this loaf in an oven from cold was born. There are instructions for this method below, and for a more conventional way of cooking the loaf for all the doubters!

you need

250 ml/9 fl oz/$1\frac{1}{8}$ cups water
2 tsp salt
2 tsp granulated sugar
100 g/$3\frac{1}{2}$ oz/$\frac{3}{4}$ cup strong wholemeal flour
350 g/12 oz/$2\frac{1}{4}$ cups very strong white bread flour
$2\frac{1}{2}$ tsp instant or fast-acting dried yeast

to make

Lightly grease a baking tray. Pour the water into the breadmaker bucket, followed by the salt and sugar. Cover the liquid with the flour and finally sprinkle the yeast over the top. Fit the bucket into the breadmaker and set to the dough programme. When the cycle is complete, turn the dough out on to a lightly floured surface and knead until smooth. Cut out one third of the dough and shape into a round. Shape the remaining two-thirds into a round loaf shape. Brush the top of the larger piece of dough with a little water and place the smaller third on top. With floured fingers, push the smaller round down through the centre of the dough to the base to seal the loaf together and create the traditional shape. Place the loaf on the baking sheet, cover with a tea towel and leave in a warm place to prove for 30 minutes. To bake the loaf in the traditional way, place the loaf in the bottom of a cold oven and turn the oven on to 190°C/375°F/gas mark 5. The loaf will rise a little more as the oven heats and will eventually bake. Cook for 30–40 minutes, depending on your oven, checking it after 30 minutes. To cook the loaf faster, bake in a preheated oven at 190°C/375°F/gas mark 5 for 25–30 minutes. Transfer to a wire rack and leave to cool.

muffins

The term muffin is thought to originate from the old French word *moufflet*, meaning soft in the context of bread. There are references to English muffins as early as 1747. The muffin peaked in popularity during the 19th century and in Victorian times muffin men could be seen carrying trays of muffins on their heads through the streets at teatime, ringing hand bells. Serving muffins is surrounded by etiquette issues. It is said that muffins should always be served fresh and never be cut in half. Instead one should snip around the edges, pull top and bottom apart and insert butter in thin slices – spreading butter squashes the delicate texture of the interior and ruins the bun.

Makes 10

you need

200 ml/7 fl oz/$^7/_8$ cup full cream milk
200 ml/7 fl oz/$^7/_8$ cup water
2 tbsp melted butter
1 tbsp granulated sugar
1 tsp salt
225 g/8 oz/$1^1/_2$ cups strong white bread flour
225 g/8 oz/$1^1/_2$ cups plain flour
$2^1/_2$ tsp instant or fast-acting dried yeast

For the finish:

a little sunflower oil
rice flour

to make

Generously sprinkle a baking tray with rice flour. Pour the milk and water into the breadmaker bucket followed by the melted butter, sugar and salt. Cover the mixture with the flour and sprinkle the yeast over the top. Fit the bucket into the breadmaker and set to the dough programme. When the cycle is complete, dust the worktop with a little rice flour, turn the dough out and knead lightly. This is quite a light and sticky dough and you will need to take care not to dry it out by adding too much rice flour when kneading. It may be helpful to use a plastic scraper when kneading. Divide the dough into 10 equally-sized pieces and shape each piece into a round flat bun. Place the buns on the baking tray and leave in a warm place to prove for about 15 minutes, until they regain their freeform shape. Be careful not to let them rise too much, or they will lose their characteristic shape while cooking. Heat a griddle or large, thick-bottomed non-stick frying pan over a medium heat. Rub a little sunflower oil over the pan. Cook the muffins in batches of 4 or 5, depending on the size of your pan or griddle. Transfer the muffins carefully to the griddle and cook for 8–10 minutes on each side until each side is biscuit-coloured, with a pale ring around the middle. The dough will firm up as it cooks, which you can check if you press lightly on the top of the muffins as they're cooking. As you cook each batch, wrap the cooked muffins in a tea towel while you cook the remainder to help keep them soft and moist. The second batch may have risen slightly more than the first but this will not jeopardize the flavour. Traditionally, muffins were toasted on each side, snipped open and served with butter (see above).

midlands

midlands

Take a map and draw a rough circle around Nottingham, Kettering, Warwick, Hereford, Shrewsbury and Cheshire and you'll have roughly outlined the Midlands. Sitting in the heart of England these mid-counties have no coastline and so the regional specialities focus solely on the yields of the land. But what riches are on offer. Despite having no sea, the region benefits from water in the spa towns of Ashbourne, Buxton and Malvern; and, as one of the prime beef and dairy cattle regions of the country, milk, cream and wonderful cheeses are plentiful too. One of the most famous of all cheeses– Stilton – is named after the village in Cambridgeshire yet produced here (see page 70). Red Leicester and Cheshire also hold national acclaim.

Worcestershire enjoys the perfect climate for fruit production from tree, vine and bush. The Worcestershire Black Pear is the county's original variety, and the famous plum varieties including Evesham Wonder, Pershore Yellow Egg and Purple Pershore, also come from here. In fact, Pershore (west of Evesham) or 'Pearshore' was the heart of pear country. Pershore Plum Day is held every August and is a mecca for plum lovers nationwide; also, the Vale of Evesham Spring Blossom Trail gives visitors to the county an excellent view of the orchards in bloom from March to May.

Salad leaves and beans are popular crops too, with asparagus production particularly significant in the region for a short season every year. It is argued that the region's asparagus is the best in the world and every May an asparagus auction is held at the Fleece Inn at Bretforton to raise funds for the local brass band. Chefs from London's most exclusive hotels are regular visitors to this event, making their journey especially to bid for the fantastic shoots.

On the arable lands oats were grown in abundance in the 18th and 19th centuries especially in Derbyshire, with the famous oatcakes an established regional delicacy. Also from Derbyshire the Bakewell Tart that, like so many great specialities, was first created by accident around 1850.

chester buns

Chester is rich in archaeological history, with the walls that were built at the time of the Roman occupation still preserved. Chester served as a centre for the shipping trade in the 13th century and its ships served Scotland, Ireland, France and Spain. Today, one of its most distinctive features is The Rows – double level walkways with a continuous line of balconies with shops at both street and first floor levels – which have been in existence since the 14th century.

Despite its wonderful history, clues to the origins of the sweet Chester Buns are scarce but stories do exist of bakers in the city delivering bread by horse-drawn van in the 1920s. Famously these bakers would generally include a large basket of penny currant buns. It's possible that the currants may have been omitted from the recipe over time to give more simple buns, with sweetened condensed milk and a sugar and water glaze added for extra richness.

Makes 8

you need

125 ml/4 fl oz/½ cup water

150 ml/5 fl oz/⅝ cup sweetened condensed milk

1 medium egg, beaten

1 tsp salt

50 g/2 oz/¼ cup very soft butter

225 g/8 oz/1½ cups very strong white bread flour

225 g/8 oz/1½ cups plain flour

2½ tsp instant or fast-acting dried yeast

For the glaze:

1 tsp caster sugar

1 tbsp water

to make

Lightly grease a baking tray. To make the buns, pour the water, condensed milk and egg into the breadmaker bucket, followed by the salt and butter. Cover the liquid with the flour and finally sprinkle the yeast over the top. Fit the bucket into the breadmaker and set to the dough programme. When the cycle is complete, turn the dough out on to a lightly floured surface and knead until smooth. Divide the dough into 8 equally sized pieces and shape each piece into a round roll. Place the buns on the baking sheet, cover with a tea towel and leave in a warm place to prove for 45 minutes. To make the glaze, whisk together the sugar and water. Brush over the proved buns and bake in a preheated oven at 200°C/400°F/gas mark 6 for 10–15 minutes until golden. Transfer to a wire rack and leave to cool.

shrewsbury 'biscuit' bread

Shrewsbury Biscuits have been made for centuries. The light, lemony biscuits were traditionally either flavoured with currants, or caraway seeds for added variety. I've transferred these distinctive flavours to the breadmaker with this wonderfully fragrant loaf. Caraway seeds give the bread a clean, slightly sharp, piquant flavour and an aroma reminiscent of anise. They are the perfect partner to the lemon which traditionally flavours this tasty bread. For a classic alternative simply add currants for a sweeter taste to complement the zesty lemon. The choice is yours – leave it simple or enhance with fruit and seeds – either way it's delicious.

you need

225 ml/8 fl oz/1 cup water
2 medium egg yolks
2 tbsp melted butter
4 tbsp caster sugar
1 tsp salt
grated rind of 2 lemons
juice of 1 lemon
450 g/16 oz/3 cups strong white bread flour
1¼ tsp instant or fast-acting dried yeast
Optional extras:
50 g/2 oz/⅜ cup currants
or
2 tbsp caraway seeds

to make

Pour the water into the breadmaker bucket, followed by the egg and butter. Cover the liquid with the sugar, salt, lemon rind, juice and the flour. Finally, sprinkle the yeast over the top. Fit the bucket into the breadmaker and set to the basic white programme. Add the currants or caraway seeds, if desired, according to your manual's instructions, usually at the beginning of the second kneading cycle or when the machine bleeps. Once cooked, carefully shake the loaf from the bucket and stand it the right way up on a wire cooling rack. Leave the bread to cool for at least an hour before cutting and/or removing the paddle if necessary.

derbyshire classics

Derbyshire plays host to some of the finest food and drink that the Midlands has to offer. Spring water flows freely from the high Peak District and it is also home to the famous Bakewell Pudding. With oats proving such a popular crop for the region, it's no surprise that Derbyshire and Staffordshire have their very own regional oatcakes, with other bakes like gingerbread and brandy snaps also popular.

bakewell bread

Derbyshire's Bakewell Pudding – not to be confused with Bakewell Tart (which locals claim to be distinctly inferior) – was first created at a Bakewell inn when a cook inadvertently spoiled a recipe for strawberry tart. The cook's mistake created such delicious results that the accidental puddings (made from a mixture of eggs, sugar, butter, almonds and jam in a pastry case) were soon made for sale. They are still produced by hand at the Old Original Bakewell Pudding Shop.

This bread takes the flavours of the traditional Bakewell Pudding and puts them into a rich yeast dough. This truly fantastic loaf makes the finest toast.

you need

225 ml/8 fl oz/1 cup water
2 medium eggs, beaten
2 tbsp double cream
1 tsp almond essence
4 tbsp raspberry jam
$1\frac{1}{2}$ tsp salt
50 g/2 oz/$\frac{3}{16}$ cup caster sugar
75 g/3 oz/$\frac{3}{4}$ cup ground almonds
450 g/16 oz/3 cups very strong white bread flour
70 g/$2\frac{1}{2}$ oz/$\frac{1}{2}$ cup plain flour
$1\frac{1}{4}$ tsp instant or fast-acting dried yeast
For the glaze:
1 egg
1 tbsp water
pinch of salt
1 tbsp flaked almonds

to make

Pour the water, eggs and cream into the breadmaker bucket, followed by the almond essence, jam, salt and sugar. Cover the mixture with the almonds and flour and finally sprinkle the yeast over the top. Fit the bucket into the breadmaker and set to the basic white programme. If you have an adjustable crust facility on your machine, select the dark setting. Forty-five minutes before the end of the cycle, whisk together the egg, water and salt to make the glaze. Carefully lift the lid of the machine and brush on the egg wash and sprinkle the flaked almonds over. Once cooked, carefully shake the loaf from the bucket and stand it the right way up on a wire cooling rack. Leave the bread to cool for at least an hour before slicing and/or removing the paddle if necessary.

derbyshire and staffordshire oatcakes

The oatcakes of Staffordshire and Derbyshire, leavened with yeast, are almost like little pancakes made of oatmeal – nothing like Scottish oatcakes which are more biscuity. With the merest hint of yeastiness, Derbyshire and Staffordshire Oatcakes lend themselves perfectly to both sweet and savoury accompaniments. Regional recipes that I have found for both vary only very slightly and purists may curse that I only quote a single recipe here to cover both counties.

Whichever county you credit for the origin of this recipe, these delicious savoury cakes can be served hot or cold. Try them for breakfast with eggs and bacon or spread with butter and jam for tea – the choice is yours.

Makes 10

you need

225 ml/8 fl oz/1 cup full cream milk

225 ml/8 fl oz/1 cup water

$^1/_2$ tsp granulated sugar

$^1/_2$ tsp salt

125 g/4 oz/$^7/_8$ cup fine oatmeal

125 g/4 oz/$^7/_8$ cup plain wholemeal flour

2 tsp instant or fast-acting dried yeast

For the finish:

vegetable oil

to make

Pour the milk and water into the breadmaker bucket, followed by the sugar and salt. Cover the liquid with the oatmeal and flour and finally sprinkle the yeast over. Fit the bucket into the breadmaker and set to the dough programme. When the cycle is complete, heat a thick-bottomed, non-stick frying pan or griddle over a medium heat. Brush the pan with a little oil. Spoon enough of the batter into the pan to give cakes about 20–23 cm/8–9 in across. If the batter is too thick to run nicely, add a little extra milk or water. As the cakes cook, the surface of each cake will become covered with tiny holes. Turn the oatcakes after about 2–3 minutes when the upper side is dry and the underside golden and cook for a further 2–3 minutes. Wrap the oatcakes in a tea towel to keep warm and serve immediately.

sticky gingerbread

One of the surprising discoveries I made while researching this book was the regional variation in gingerbread recipes. Most commonly known gingerbreads are like the one below – light, sticky and sweet. But as we travel further north the ingredients and texture change and the recipe becomes much denser – more similar to Parkin – with the addition of oatmeal and sometimes even fruit and nuts, too. If, like me, you're a big fan of gingerbread you'll also enjoy the other regional variations in this book – see pages 102 and 152.

you need

125 g/4 oz/1/2 cup butter
125 g/4 oz/3/4 cup soft light brown sugar
50 g/2 oz/1/8 cup golden syrup
75 g/3 oz/3/16 cup black treacle
175 g/6 oz/1 1/8 cups plain flour
1 tsp ground ginger
1 tsp ground cinnamon
150 ml/5 fl oz/5/8 cup semi-skimmed milk, warmed
1 tsp bicarbonate of soda
1 medium egg, beaten
1 1/2 tbsp chopped glacé ginger

to make

Put the butter, sugar, syrup and treacle into a saucepan and heat gently until the sugar has dissolved and the butter has melted. Do not let it boil. Pour into the breadmaker bucket and cover the mixture with the flour and spices. Stir the bicarbonate of soda into the warm milk and add this to the mix, together with the beaten egg and ginger. Fit the bucket into the breadmaker and set to the cake programme. After 5 minutes of the mixing cycle, scrape down the sides of the bucket with a plastic spatula to ensure all the ingredients are evenly mixed. When cooked, remove the bucket from the machine and leave the cake for 5–10 minutes to cool. Carefully shake the cake from the bucket and stand it the right way up on a wire cooling rack. Leave to cool.

fine british cheese

The westerly counties of the Midlands are prime dairy cattle locations and the source of the raw material for some of Britain's finest cheese. Stilton is one of the few British cheeses to be granted the status of 'protected designation origin' by the EC. This states that only cheese produced to a strict code in the counties of Derbyshire, Leicestershire and Nottinghamshire can be called Stilton.

shropshire blue quiche

Though essentially of French origin, quiches made with a yeast-leavened dough base started to feature in the most popular eateries here in the 19th century and following this, adaptations of the classics soon made it into British recipe books. Here, I've used the traditional thin dough crust, and a new delicate and light filling featuring the local creamy, smooth Shropshire Blue cheese.

you need

2 large eggs, beaten
6 tbsp soured cream
1 tsp sugar
2 tsp salt
250 g/9 oz/1¾ cups plain flour
2 tsp instant or fast-acting dried yeast

For the filling:
6 tbsp milk
3 large eggs, beaten
3 tbsp soured cream
150 g/5¼ oz/1¼ cups crumbled Shropshire Blue cheese
pinch of grated nutmeg
salt and pepper, to taste

to make

To make the dough, pour the eggs into the breadmaker bucket, followed by the cream, sugar and salt. Cover the mixture with the flour and sprinkle the yeast over the top. Fit the bucket into the breadmaker and set to the dough programme. After 10 minutes of the mixing cycle, scrape down the sides of the bucket with a plastic spatula to ensure all the ingredients are evenly mixed. When the cycle is complete, turn the dough out on to a lightly floured surface and knead until smooth. Roll the dough out to fit a 20 cm/8 in pie dish. Leave the edges untrimmed for now.

To make the filling, mix the milk, eggs, soured cream, cheese, nutmeg and salt and pepper together and pour into the dough-lined dish. Trim the edges of the dough. Bake the quiche in a preheated oven at 220°C/425°F/gas mark 7 for 15 minutes. Reduce the heat to 190°C/375°F/gas mark 5 and bake for a further 10 minutes, until the quiche is golden and the filling is just set. Remove the quiche from the oven and serve either warm or cold.

cheshire cheese and asparagus wraps

In this recipe there is a perfect marriage between two classic regional specialities: Cheshire cheese and the delicate asparagus that is grown in the Vale of Evesham. Somehow the mellow saltiness of melted Cheshire cheese brings out the best in the succulent asparagus which, when held together in a light dough crust, makes an elegant idea for a starter, snack or finger buffet.

Makes 16

you need

300 ml/11 fl oz/1⅜ cups water

1 tbsp sunflower oil

1½ tsp salt

1 tsp sugar

450 g/16 oz/3 cups very strong white bread flour

2½ tsp instant or fast-acting dried yeast

For the filling:

16 asparagus tips

3 spring onions, thinly sliced

100 g/3½ oz/¾ cup grated Cheshire cheese

salt and freshly ground black pepper

1 egg, beaten

to make

Lightly grease a baking tray. Pour the water into the breadmaker bucket, followed by the oil, salt and sugar. Cover the liquid with the flour and sprinkle the yeast over the top. Fit the bucket into the breadmaker and set to the dough programme. Blanch the asparagus tips in boiling water for 2 minutes. Cool them rapidly in cold water. Drain and set aside. When the cycle is complete, turn the dough out on to a lightly floured surface and knead until smooth. Divide the dough into 16 equally-sized pieces and roll each piece into a circle about the size of a saucer. Place a piece of asparagus in the centre of each circle so that the tip falls just above the rim. Sprinkle the cheese and onions over the centre of each circle on top of the asparagus, leaving the rim of the circle uncovered. Season the filling of each wrap with salt and pepper. Brush the edges of the circle with beaten egg and fold up the bottom of each wrap. Next fold the sides into the centre to achieve the classic wrap shape, sealing in the filling apart from the asparagus tip. Place the wraps on to the baking sheet and bake in a preheated oven at 220°C/425°F/gas mark 7 for 8–10 minutes until puffy and golden. Serve hot.

crumpets

When I first embarked on making crumpets, I have to admit I wasn't that hopeful that I would get good results. However, once I'd researched the subject a little I was prepared to give it a go and I have to say my work was rewarded with many a jolly tasting session. I found that by making one large pan sized crumpet I not only did away with the fuss and bother of trying to release individual crumpets from their rings halfway through cooking, but also saved the usual performance of someone eating their breakfast next to the toaster while the others sit down and wait for the shifts of individually toasted crumpets. I discovered that with the breadmaker's automatic timer, I can time the batter to be ready just before breakfast so all I have to do is stir in the bicarbonate of soda mix, make a cup of tea and turn out a very impressive crumpet with very little effort – I am hooked!

Serves 4–6

you need

150 ml/5 fl oz/$\frac{5}{8}$ cup semi-skimmed milk
150 ml/5 fl oz/$\frac{5}{8}$ cup water
1 tbsp sunflower oil
$\frac{1}{2}$ tsp salt
$\frac{1}{2}$ tsp granulated sugar
125 g/4 oz/$\frac{7}{8}$ cup plain flour
125 g/4 oz/$\frac{7}{8}$ cup very strong white bread flour
1$\frac{1}{2}$ tsp instant or fast-acting dried yeast
$\frac{1}{2}$ tsp bicarbonate of soda
75 ml/3 fl oz/$\frac{3}{8}$ cup water, warmed

For the finish:

oil

to make

Pour the milk, water and oil into the breadmaker, followed by the salt and sugar. Cover the liquid with the flour and sprinkle the yeast over the top. Fit the bucket into the breadmaker and set to the dough programme. When the cycle is complete, the batter should have risen slightly and have a bubbly texture. Depending on your breadmaker, it may be necessary to remove the bucket from the machine at the end of the programme and allow a further 30 minutes in a warm place before the batter has risen and become bubbly. Mix the bicarbonate of soda with the warm water and pour into the batter. Stir in with a plastic spatula. Leave the batter for a few more minutes until it starts to froth. Heat a heavy based frying pan, approximately 24 cm/9$\frac{1}{2}$in across, over a medium heat until thoroughly warmed. Brush the pan with the oil and pour in the bubbling batter. Turn the heat to its lowest and leave to cook. As the crumpet cooks, little bubbles will appear all over the surface and gradually these will turn into holes as the batter sets. Don't expect your homemade crumpets to be as evenly holey as commercially produced ones, but you should have enough holes to get that characteristic look. After about 20–25 minutes, the batter should have set on the surface. At this point remove the pan from the heat and leave for 10 minutes to cool. Toast the crumpet under the grill, cut into wedges and serve immediately with butter and jam.

rice bread

Rice was originally used as a dough extender as, by adding rice, economic cooks could make more bread from the same amount of flour. However, rice bread soon became renowned for its moistness and excellent keeping qualities and in the 19th century it was the favoured choice for sandwiches as it was thought to be the best bread for preventing the fillings from drying out. This traditional recipe uses cooked long grain rice to produce a moist and versatile loaf. Why does this recipe appear in the Midlands? Think of the curry houses and Birmingham's multi-cultural society and it's no surprise to discover that the Midlands is the UK's biggest regional consumer of rice.

you need

225 ml/8 fl oz/1 cup boiling water
75 g/3 oz/3/8 cup easy-cook long grain rice
225 ml/8 fl oz/1 cup water
2 tsp salt
2 tsp granulated sugar
450 g/16 oz/3 cups strong white bread flour
1½ tsp instant or fast-acting dried yeast

to make

Cook the rice in the boiling water until it is soft and all the water has been absorbed. Leave the rice to cool slightly and then pour into the breadmaker bucket. Add the second cup of water, the salt and then the sugar. Cover the mixture with the flour and finally sprinkle the yeast over the top. Fit the bucket into the breadmaker and set to the basic white programme. Once cooked, carefully shake the loaf from the bucket and stand it the right way up on a wire cooling rack. Leave the bread to cool for at least an hour before slicing and/or removing the paddle if necessary.

red leicester bread sticks

The medium-strong flavour of Red Leicester cheese is perfect for these crispy breadsticks which make an excellent nibble to serve with drinks. For extra zing, try sprinkling them with chilli flakes before baking.

Makes 30–40

you need

250 ml/9 fl oz/1⅛ cups water

3 tbsp olive oil

2 tsp sugar

1 tsp salt

½ tsp paprika

½ tsp mustard powder

75 g/3 oz/1 cup grated Red Leicester cheese

2 tbsp semolina

450 g/16 oz/3 cups strong white bread flour

2½ tsp instant or fast-acting dried yeast

For the finish:

semolina

For the glaze:

1 egg yolk

1 tbsp water

pinch of salt

For the topping (optional):

dried chilli flakes

to make

Lightly grease a baking tray and dust with semolina. To make the dough, pour the water and oil into the breadmaker bucket, followed by the sugar and salt. Sprinkle the paprika, mustard, cheese, semolina and flour over the top and, finally, add the yeast. Fit the bucket into the breadmaker and set to the dough programme. When the cycle is complete, turn the dough out on to a lightly floured surface and knead until smooth. Divide the dough into 30–40 equall- sized pieces. Shape each piece into a round shape and then an oval. Continue to roll the oval, running your fingers along the dough to form very thin sticks about 25cm/10 in long. Place the sticks 1cm/½ in apart on the baking sheet. To make the glaze, whisk together the egg, water and salt. Brush the sticks with the glaze and sprinkle with the chilli flakes, if desired. Bake in a preheated oven at 200ºC/400ºF/gas mark 6 for 15–20 minutes until crisp and golden. Transfer to a wire rack and leave to cool.

jam doughnuts

Here's a breadmaker recipe for the classic jam doughnut – light, fluffy and filled with strawberry jam. If you love doughnuts and you'd like to try something a little different, see also the recipe for Isle of Wight Doughnuts on page 53.

Makes 10

you need

225 ml/8 fl oz/1 cup semi-skimmed milk

2 large eggs, beaten

75 ml/3 fl oz/3/8 cup melted butter

1 tbsp granulated sugar

225 g/8 oz/1 1/2 cups plain flour

225 g/8 oz/1 1/2 cups very strong white bread flour

2 1/2 tsp instant or fast-acting dried yeast

For the finish:

150 g/5 1/4 oz/1/2 cup strawberry jam

1 egg, beaten

oil

caster sugar

to make

Pour the milk into the breadmaker bucket, followed by the eggs and butter. Cover the mixture with the sugar and flour and then sprinkle the yeast over the top. Fit the bucket into the breadmaker and set to the dough programme. When the cycle is complete, turn the dough out on to a lightly floured board and knead until smooth. Divide the dough into 20 equally-sized pieces and roll each into a flat round. Place a teaspoonful of jam on to the centre of 10 of the pieces of dough and brush beaten egg onto the plain dough around it. Cover each piece with a plain circle of dough and seal the edges. Shape each one into a flat round bun. Cover the doughnuts with a tea towel. Pre-heat the deep fat fryer or half fill a wok with oil and heat on the hob until very hot. Fry the doughnuts, a few at a time, for approximately 8 minutes, turning if necessary, until puffy and golden. Drain them on kitchen paper and dust with caster sugar to serve.

the north

the north

The lands bounded by Manchester, Merseyside and Yorkshire in the south and Britain's northern extremities of Cumbria and Northumberland form, roughly, the area known as the North of England. This region contains dramatic coastline and bustling seaside towns while inland peaceful rolling moors and lakes can be found under heather-covered hills and craggy mountains. With many old industrial centres here, food has developed around hard-working communities living in a harsh climate. Simple, cheap and tasty dishes frame this region's cuisine where, for centuries, cooks have found inventive ways to ensure that nothing was wasted.

Yorkshire, Cumbria and Lancashire play host to herds of cattle and sheep in the more fertile lowlands, producing the milk and cream needed for some of the country's most famous cheese. The buttery, rich Lancashire cheese and the famous Wensleydale – eaten locally with a slice of apple pie, gingerbread or fruitcake – both originate from the region.

Despite its harsh climate, the North produces both fresh fruit and vegetables, especially hardier crops such as potatoes, carrots and parsnips. Forced rhubarb and gooseberries are also important to the area. So famous is this part of England for gooseberries that the annual Gooseberry Show at Egton Bridge in North Yorkshire gives prizes to the best and largest berries from the region.

Baking has always been important here. Wholesome and energy-rich recipes like Preston Gingerbread (page 102) and Westmorland Pepper Cake (opposite) form the backbone of the region and are often washed down with one of the region's ales.

Today this area enjoys the benefits of tourism and has a thriving network of independent producers who are making the most out of traditional recipes. You'll find shops specialising in everything from Sticky Toffee Pudding (page 96) to Windermere Cakes (page 105) and meat dishes aplenty.

westmorland pepper cake

Westmorland was a county situated between Northumberland and Cumbria. In the 1970s it became part of Northumbria and Cumbria. This is a traditional recipe from this old region and while adding pepper to a cake seems curious, it gives an interesting extra dimension to this spiced fruit loaf.

you need

75 g/3 oz/½ cup raisins
75 g/3 oz/½ cup currants
100 g/3½ oz/⁷⁄₁₆ cup caster sugar
75 g/3 oz/⁵⁄₁₆ cup butter
150 ml/5 fl oz/⅝ cup water
½ tsp ground ginger
½ tsp finely ground black pepper
1 large egg, beaten
4 tbsp full cream milk
225 g/8 oz/1½ cups self-raising flour
1 tsp baking powder

to make

Put the fruit, sugar, butter and water into a saucepan and bring to the boil. Turn the heat down and let the mixture simmer for 10 minutes. Leave to cool slightly (for about 5 minutes). Pour the fruit mixture into the breadmaker bucket, followed by the spices, egg and milk. Cover the mixture with the flour and baking powder. Fit the bucket into the breadmaker and set to the cake programme. After 5 minutes of the mixing cycle, scrape down the mixture on the sides of the bucket with a plastic spatula to ensure all the ingredients are evenly mixed. When cooked, remove the bucket from the machine and leave to cool for 5 minutes. Carefully shake the loaf from the bucket and stand it the right way up on a wire cooling rack. Leave to cool.

sticky toffee pudding

Whether accredited to Yorkshire or Cumbria, there's no doubt that this has become one of Britain's favourite puddings. Light and airy, incredibly sweet and sticky, there's nothing quite like sticky toffee pudding topped with rich toffee sauce. With a breadmaker it's extremely quick and easy to make without tying up the oven and, once you've tried it, you'll soon be coming back for more.

you need

175 g/6 oz/$1\frac{1}{4}$ cups stoned and chopped dates
300 ml/11 fl oz/$1\frac{3}{8}$ cups water
1 tsp bicarbonate of soda
$3\frac{1}{2}$ tbsp melted butter
175 g/6 oz/$1\frac{1}{4}$ cups dark soft brown sugar
2 medium eggs, beaten
190 g/$6\frac{1}{2}$ oz/$1\frac{1}{4}$ cups self-raising flour
1 tsp vanilla extract
For the sauce:
250 ml/9 fl oz/$1\frac{1}{8}$ cups double cream
50 g/2 oz/$\frac{1}{4}$ cup demerara sugar
2 tbsp black treacle

to make

To make the pudding, put the dates and water in a saucepan and bring to the boil. Simmer for approximately 5 minutes until soft. Remove the dates from the heat, leave to cool slightly for 2–3 minutes and stir in the bicarbonate of soda. Pour into the breadmaker bucket and add the butter, sugar, eggs, flour and vanilla. Fit the bucket into the breadmaker and set to the cake programme. After 5 minutes of the mixing cycle, scrape down the sides of the bucket with a plastic spatula to ensure all the ingredients are evenly mixed. A few minutes before the pudding is ready, prepare the sauce by gently melting all the ingredients together over a low heat. Stir well to ensure all the ingredients have blended together and slowly bring to the boil. When the breadmaker cycle is complete, gently turn the cake out onto a serving plate and serve immediately with the sauce. If you want to eat the pudding later, it reheats well in the microwave. Always make the sauce just before serving.

lancashire's larder

While the industrial heritage of Lancashire cannot be ignored, the region has also given us one of the nation's finest cheeses. Farmhouse Lancashire Cheese was first made in 1913 and is traditionally served as an accompaniment to apples and as a favourite partner of local gingerbread. Originally made from milk collected over 2 days' milkings, traditional farmhouse varieties are still salted and cut by hand.

breadmaker eccles cakes

Eccles Cakes are undoubtedly Lancashire's most famous bake and they traditionally comprise a flaky pastry case surrounding a mixture of fruit, sugar and spice. This is an adaptation of the original recipe that replaces the puff pastry with a sweet yeast dough.

Makes 6–8

you need

125 ml/4 fl oz/$\frac{1}{2}$ cup semi-skimmed milk
125 ml/4 fl oz/$\frac{1}{2}$ cup water
1 large egg yolk, beaten
3 tbsp melted butter
4 tbsp granulated sugar
1 tsp salt
450 g/16 oz/3 cups very strong white bread flour
$1\frac{1}{2}$ tsp instant or fast-acting dried yeast

For the filling:

50 ml/2 fl oz/$\frac{1}{4}$ cup melted butter
150 g/$5\frac{1}{4}$ oz/1 cup currants
1 tbsp mixed peel
75 g/3 oz/$\frac{7}{16}$ cup demerara sugar
$\frac{3}{4}$ tsp mixed spice

For the glaze:

1 egg
1 tbsp water
pinch of salt
caster sugar

to make

Pour the milk, water, egg yolk and butter into the breadmaker bucket. Add the sugar, salt and flour, then sprinkle on the yeast. Fit the bucket into the breadmaker and set to the dough programme. When complete, turn the dough out on to a lightly-floured surface and knead until smooth. Roll out as thinly as possible and cut 6–8 circles using a saucer as a guide. Mix together the butter, currants, peel, sugar and spice and spoon into the centre of each circle. Brush the edges with water and bring up over the filling, pinching together. Turn each cake over and gently flatten with a rolling pin. Cut three slashes in the top of each cake and put on to a lightly greased baking tray. Whisk together the egg, water and salt and brush the glaze over the buns, sprinkle with caster sugar. Bake in a preheated oven at 200°C/400°F/gas mark 6 for 10–15 minutes.

lancashire cheese and apple cake

Lancashire Cheese and Apple Cake is a traditional cake of the region and I've found that the combination of flavours and textures transfers perfectly to a yeast dough in this attractive and versatile bake. Bittersweet fresh apple melts perfectly into the raisin-studded rich sweet dough, providing just the right balance of texture and flavour to host the creamy Lancashire Cheese. It's particularly delicious served warm.

you need

2 large egg yolks, beaten
75 ml/3 fl oz/$^{3}/_{8}$ cup apple juice
75 ml/3 fl oz/$^{3}/_{8}$ cup semi-skimmed milk
3 tbsp melted butter
2 tbsp water
$1^{1}/_{2}$ tsp salt
50 g/2 oz/$^{1}/_{4}$ cup demerara sugar
$^{1}/_{2}$ tsp grated nutmeg
100 g/$3^{1}/_{2}$ oz/1 cup finely chopped dessert apple
70 g/$2^{1}/_{2}$ oz/$^{1}/_{2}$ cup strong wholemeal bread flour
375 g/13 oz/$2^{1}/_{2}$ cups very strong white bread flour
$2^{1}/_{2}$ tsp instant or fast-acting dried yeast
100 g/$3^{1}/_{2}$ oz/$^{5}/_{8}$ cup raisins

For the filling:

150 g/$5^{1}/_{4}$ oz/$1^{1}/_{4}$ cup crumbled Lancashire cheese

For the glaze:

1 egg
1 tbsp water
pinch of salt
1 dessert apple, cored, quartered and thinly sliced

to make

Lightly grease a loose-bottomed 23 cm/9 in cake tin. To make the dough, pour the egg yolks, apple juice, milk, water and butter into the breadmaker bucket. Add the salt, sugar, nutmeg and apple. Cover the mixture with the flour and sprinkle the yeast over the top. Fit the bucket into the breadmaker and set to the dough programme. Add the raisins according to your manual's instructions, usually at the beginning of the second kneading cycle or when the machine bleeps. When the cycle is complete, turn the dough out on to a lightly floured surface and knead until smooth. Divide the dough in half and roll each piece out into a circle 23 cm/9 in across. Spread the cheese evenly over one circle, leaving 2.5cm/1 in around the edge. Brush the edges of the circle with water and place the other circle on top, pinching them together to seal. Carefully place the bake in the cake tin. Cover with a tea towel and leave to prove in a warm place until doubled in size. To make the glaze, whisk together the egg, water and salt. Brush over the proved dough and garnish with the slices of apple. Glaze again, ensuring the apple is also coated. Bake in a preheated oven at 200°C/400°F/gas mark 6 for 30 minutes until golden. Serve either hot or cold.

preston gingerbread

Although Grasmere Gingerbread cannot be produced well in a breadmaker, you can make Preston Gingerbread with excellent results. As with many northern cakes like Parkin, this gingerbread is much denser and drier than the stickier versions associated with the south of England (see recipe on page 82). It was probably made like this to ensure it kept well and improved with age – these hard working communities did not have time to bake cakes that would go off after a couple of days. Preston Gingerbread is best kept in an airtight tin for 2–3 days before eating. For a traditional approach, try serving it with Lancashire cheese and apples.

you need

350 g/12 oz/2 1/4 cups plain flour
1 tsp ground ginger
pinch of grated nutmeg
pinch of mixed spice
75 g/3 oz/5/16 cup soft butter
225 g/8 oz/5/8 cup black treacle
75 ml/3 fl oz/3/8 cup semi-skimmed milk, warmed
1 tsp bicarbonate of soda
1 large egg, beaten

to make

Put the flour and spices into a bowl and rub in the butter until the mixture resembles fine breadcrumbs. In a saucepan, gently heat the treacle until it runs free from a spoon. Do not boil. Stir the bicarbonate of soda into the warm milk. Pour the treacle into the breadmaker bucket, followed by the milk mixture and the beaten egg. Cover the liquid with the flour mixture. Fit the bucket into the breadmaker and set to the cake programme. After 5 minutes of the mixing cycle, scrape down the sides of the bucket with a plastic spatula to ensure all the ingredients are evenly mixed. When cooked, carefully shake the loaf from the bucket and stand it the right way up on a wire cooling rack. When cool, place in an airtight container. Ideally you should leave it for 2–3 days before eating.

moors and dales

Traditionally, Yorkshire was a harsh place to live. Farming on the bleak dales was hard and only the toughest breeds of sheep and pigs could live on the land. Pork, mutton and sheep's milk were important staples of the rural diet and every part of the animal was used in regional dishes, to ensure nothing was wasted.

The farmhouse range was the boiler house for farm workers – the essential centre from which all sustaining foods would be produced. Frequently there would be a cauldron of stew suspended over the hearth and flat bakestones on the side for producing oatcakes and varieties of bread and scones. Old favourites included 'haver' bread or 'clapbread' made from fermented oatmeal and milk, and Parkin that was usually cooked once the oven had cooled slightly after baking the bread. On the lowlands, milk was plentiful and it is this that made the now famous Wensleydale cheese. Fresh milk is also one of the prime ingredients in the area's most famous dish – Yorkshire Pudding.

yorkshire breakfast bread

This regional Yorkshire loaf is made only with the natural fat found in the milk and therefore is best eaten on the day it's baked. Made with a mix of white and wholemeal flour this is a pleasingly rustic loaf with a light texture and wholesome taste. As you would expect from a breakfast bread, it makes wonderful toast.

you need

275 ml/10 fl oz/1¼ cups full cream milk

1 tsp granulated sugar

1 tsp salt

225 g/8 oz/1½ cups strong wholemeal bread flour

225 g/8 oz/1½ cups very strong white bread flour

1½ tsp instant or fast-acting dried yeast

to make

Pour the milk into the breadmaker bucket, followed by the sugar and salt. Cover the mixture with the flour and finally sprinkle the yeast over the top. Fit the bucket into the breadmaker and set to the basic white programme. Once cooked, carefully shake the loaf from the bucket and stand it the right way up on a wire cooling rack. Leave the bread to cool for at least an hour before slicing and/or removing the paddle if necessary.

yorkshire teacakes

Here's a breadmaker recipe for this most popular Yorkshire treat. These rich, fruity spiced buns are flavoured with nutmeg and cinnamon and are particularly aromatic when served toasted, with lashings of butter.

Makes 8

you need

75 ml/3 fl oz/⅜ cup water

150 ml/5 fl oz/⅝ cup semi-skimmed milk

1 large egg, beaten

3 tbsp melted butter

½ tsp salt

50 g/2 oz/3/16 cup caster sugar

½ tsp grated nutmeg

½ tsp ground cinnamon

70 g/2½ oz/½ cup strong wholemeal bread flour

375 g/13 oz/2½ cups very strong white bread flour

2½ tsp instant or fast-acting dried yeast

50 g/2 oz/¼ cup mixed peel

100 g/3½ oz/⅝ cup raisins

For the glaze:

1 egg

1 tbsp water

pinch of salt

caster sugar

to make

Lightly grease a baking tray. To make the tea cakes, pour the water, milk, egg and butter into the breadmaker bucket, followed by the salt, sugar and spices. Cover the mixture with the flour and finally sprinkle the yeast over the top. Fit the bucket into the breadmaker and set to the dough programme. Add the peel and raisins according to your manual's instructions, usually at the beginning of the second kneading cycle or when the machine bleeps. When the cycle is complete, turn the dough out on to a lightly floured surface and knead until smooth. Divide the dough into 8 equally-sized pieces and shape each piece into a round cake. Put the tea cakes onto the baking sheet and cover with a tea towel. Leave in a warm place to prove until doubled in size. To make the glaze, whisk together the egg, water and salt. Brush the glaze over the teacakes and sprinkle them with caster sugar. Bake in a preheated oven at 200°C/400°F/gas mark 6 for 12–15 minutes until golden. Serve toasted and buttered.

the lakes

Cumbria is home to Beatrix Potter and the Lake District and enjoys an abundance of traditional British foods. Comfort food is important to an area like this for energy and sustenance, and so it's no surprise that the area's specialities include many sweet dishes and confections.

windermere cakes

These cakes are reminiscent of Eccles cakes. They make the ideal sweet treat for a packed lunch or picnic and I'm sure have been enjoyed by many as they stand on the banks of Lake Windermere.

Makes 8

you need

450 g/16 oz/3 cups strong white bread flour
125 g/4 oz/½ cup hard white vegetable fat
75 g/3 oz/5/16 cup butter
350 ml/12 fl oz/1½ cups full cream milk
50 g/2 oz/5/16 cup granulated sugar
1 tsp salt
2½ tsp instant or fast-acting dried yeast

For the filling:

1 tbsp brandy or rum (optional)
50 g/2 oz/3/16 cup granulated sugar
50 g/2 oz/5/16 cup currants

For the finish and glaze:

1 egg
1 tbsp water
pinch of salt

to make

Lightly grease a baking tray. To make the dough, put the flour into a bowl and rub in the fats until the mixture resembles fine breadcrumbs. Pour the milk into the breadmaker bucket, followed by the sugar and salt. Cover the liquid with the flour mixture and sprinkle the yeast over the top. Fit the bucket into the breadmaker and set to the dough programme. To make the filling, mix together the sugar, currants and the brandy or rum, if desired, in a bowl and set aside. When the cycle is complete, turn the dough out on to a lightly floured surface and knead until smooth. Divide the dough into 16 equally sized pieces and roll each piece out into a round shape, about the size of a small saucer. Divide the filling mixture among 8 of the rounds, placing it in the centre of each one, to within 1.5 cm/½ in of the edges, leaving a clean rim of dough. To make the glaze, whisk together the egg, water and salt. Brush the glaze over the edges of the dough on each of the 8 rounds and place the remaining dough circles on top, over the filling. Press the edges firmly together to seal. Transfer the cakes to the baking sheet and cover with a tea towel. Leave in a warm place to prove for 30 minutes. Brush the cakes with the glaze and place in a preheated oven at 220°C/425°F/gas mark 7 and then immediately turn the oven down to 200°C/400°F/gas mark 6 and bake for 12–15 minutes until well risen and golden.

cumbrian christmas bread

This delicious celebration loaf contains succulent fruit, fragrant peel and just a hint of spice. It's enriched with eggs and full cream milk and sweetened with treacle – a lovely combination that is synonymous with celebration breads.

you need

1 medium egg, beaten
150 ml/5 fl oz/$^{5}/_{8}$ cup full cream milk
75 ml/3 fl oz/$^{3}/_{8}$ cup water
25 ml/1 fl oz/$^{1}/_{8}$ cup melted butter
2 tsp black treacle
75 g/3 oz/$^{5}/_{16}$ cup caster sugar
1 tsp mixed spice
1 tsp salt
225 g/8 oz/1$^{1}/_{2}$ cups very strong white bread flour
225 g/8 oz/1$^{1}/_{2}$ cups plain flour
1$^{1}/_{4}$ tsp instant or fast-acting dried yeast
25 g/1 oz/$^{1}/_{8}$ cup currants
50 g/2 oz/$^{1}/_{4}$ cup sultanas
1 tbsp mixed peel

to make

Pour the egg, milk, water, butter and treacle into the breadmaker bucket, followed by the sugar, spice and salt. Cover the mixture with the flour and sprinkle the yeast over the top. Fit the bucket into the breadmaker and set to the basic white programme. Add the currants, sultanas and peel according to your manual's instructions, usually at the beginning of the second kneading cycle or when the machine bleeps. Once cooked, carefully shake the loaf from the bucket and stand it the right way up on a wire cooling rack. Leave the bread to cool for at least an hour before slicing and/or removing the paddle if necessary.

northumbrian harvest tea cake

This Northumbrian fruited tea bread was originally made as a treat to celebrate harvest and along with the local versions of lardy cake (page 22) was sold in northern bakeries or made at home every week. Enriched with full cream milk and butter – which were plentiful in farming communities – the bread was sweetened with currants and flavoured with spice to produce a delicious tea-time treat.

you need

1 large egg, beaten
200 ml/7 fl oz/$\frac{7}{8}$ cup full cream milk
50 ml/2 fl oz/$\frac{1}{4}$ cup melted butter
$\frac{1}{2}$ tsp grated nutmeg
$\frac{1}{2}$ tsp salt
25 g/1 oz/$\frac{1}{16}$ cup granulated sugar
450 g/16 oz/3 cups very strong white bread flour
$2\frac{1}{2}$ tsp instant or fast-acting dried yeast
25 g/1 oz/$\frac{1}{8}$ cup currants
2 tbsp mixed peel

For the glaze:
1 egg
1 tbsp water
pinch of salt

to make

Lightly grease a baking tray. To make the cake, pour the egg, milk and butter into the breadmaker bucket, followed by the nutmeg, salt and sugar. Cover the mixture with the flour and sprinkle the yeast over the top. Fit the bucket into the breadmaker and set to the dough programme. Add the currants and peel according to your manual's instructions, usually at the beginning of the second kneading cycle or when the machine bleeps. Once the cycle is complete, turn the dough out on to a lightly floured surface and knead until smooth. Divide the dough into 3 equally sized pieces and shape each piece into a long rope. Plait the 3 ropes together to make a traditional plaited loaf shape. Pinch the ends together to seal and tuck them under. Transfer the loaf to the baking sheet, cover with a tea towel and leave in a warm place to prove until doubled in size. To make the glaze, whisk together the egg, water and salt. Brush over the cake and bake in a preheated oven at 190°C/375°F/gas mark 5 for 30–35 minutes. When cooked, the loaf should be golden brown and sound hollow when tapped underneath.

northumberland twists

These twisted pieces of rich, sweet dough are fun to make and are excellent for drinks parties and nibbles. They were probably made from scraps of bread dough with the sherry and sugar glaze added to transform them into little sweet treats.

you need

100 ml/$3\frac{1}{2}$ fl oz/$\frac{7}{16}$ cup melted butter

150 ml/5 fl oz/$\frac{5}{8}$ cup water

$\frac{1}{2}$ tsp salt

50 g/2 oz/$\frac{3}{16}$ cup caster sugar

450 g/16 oz/3 cups strong white bread flour

2 tsp instant or fast-acting dried yeast

For the glaze:

2 tbsp sherry

caster sugar

to make

Lightly grease a baking tray. To make the twists, pour the melted butter and water into the breadmaker bucket, followed by the salt and sugar. Cover the liquid with the flour and finally sprinkle the yeast over the top. Fit the bucket into the breadmaker and set to the dough programme. When the cycle is complete, turn the dough out on to a lightly floured surface and knead until smooth. Roll out the dough to a thickness of about $\frac{1}{2}$ cm/$\frac{1}{4}$ in and then cut strips approximately 10 cm/4 in by 1 cm/$\frac{1}{2}$ in wide. Twist each strip of dough slightly and place on to the baking sheet. To glaze the twists, brush with the sherry and sprinkle over the caster sugar. Bake in a preheated oven at 190°C/375°F/gas mark 5 for 10–15 minutes until golden.

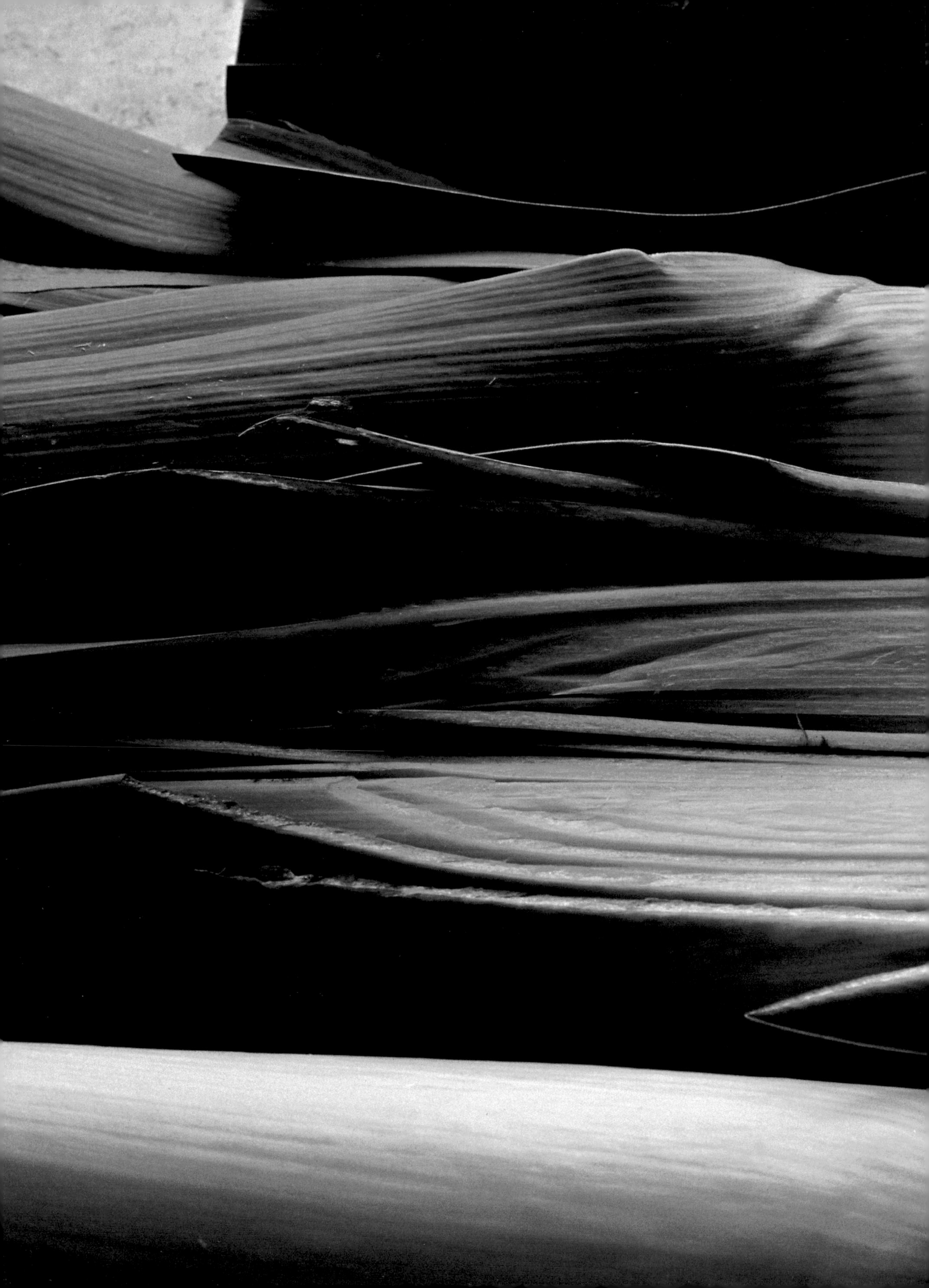

wales

wales

The Welsh border can be roughly defined with a line on a map from Monmouth to Wrexham. To the left of this line is Wales which is just 60 miles wide and 160 miles long. Inside its boundaries lie the cities of Cardiff and Swansea and in the north Mount Snowdon towers over the popular destinations of Bangor and Caernarfon while, to the south, you will find the Cardigan Bay.

Throughout history, the beautiful, rugged terrain of Wales has been a challenge for agriculture. In the north the craggy mountains will support little else but oats and sheep with classic recipes like Cacen Gneifio (Shearing Cake, page 116) and Cawl (a traditional soup made with lamb, leeks and cabbage) bearing testament to the success of sheep farming here. Oats, too, are prevalent in cooking, with Crempog (pancakes) often made and served with lashing of salty Welsh butter. Dairy cattle are kept in the low lying fields and, as well as butter, they provide the all-important cream for the famous Welsh cheeses like Caerphilly and Y Fenni.

For those that didn't earn a living from farming, quarrying or mining there was work in harvesting the food of the sea. In times now long gone, fishing for herring, mackerel, cockles and oysters was a major industry along the varied coastline of Wales. Deep mountain lakes and clear rivers also meant that freshwater fish were prevalent. From coracles – traditional small boats made from a willow framework covered with canvas or hide – fishermen would cast their nets to catch salmon and sea trout, locally called sewin.

The Welsh tea remains a famous tradition and is usually served at four in the afternoon. Here we find some of the country's most famous bakes – Bara Brith (the speckled bread, page 114) was in fact originally a rich fruit bread, and Teisen Lap (page 120) was the traditional Welsh fruitcake. Also included at tea time are many griddle cakes which were traditionally baked on a stone, flat iron or slate. Among the favourites of this kind of bread were the bakestone bread Bara Planc (page 117) and Pikelets (opposite) that are like little griddled crumpets.

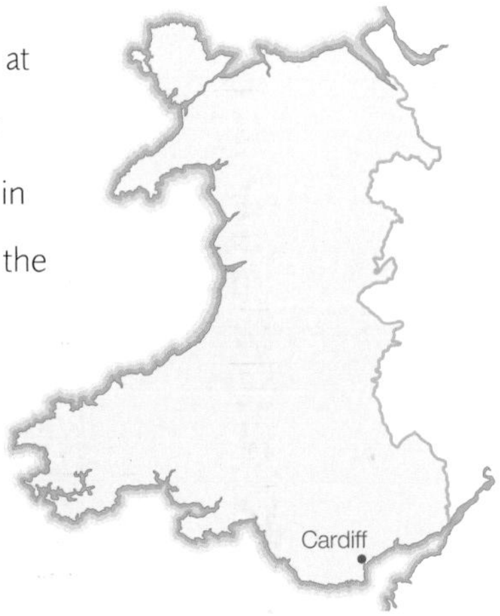

Cardiff

the famous welsh tea

There's a strong following in Wales for the traditional Welsh tea and happily many of its most popular dishes are suited to the breadmaker.

pikelets

Bara Pyglyd or Pikelets are soft griddle cakes with a texture just made for soaking up lashings of salty Welsh butter. They were traditionally served as a part of the Welsh tea and cooked on a griddle, slate or stone over an open fire.

Serves 4

you need

2 medium eggs, beaten
350 ml/12 fl oz/1½ cups full cream milk
50 ml/2 fl oz/¼ cup melted butter
2 tsp granulated sugar
pinch of salt
225 g/8 oz/1½ cups very strong white bread flour
225 g/8 oz/1½ cups plain flour
2½ tsp instant or fast-acting dried yeast
For the finish:
vegetable oil

to make

Pour the eggs, milk and butter into the breadmaker bucket, followed by the sugar and salt. Cover the mixture with the flour and finally sprinkle the yeast over the top. Fit the bucket into the breadmaker and set to the dough programme. When the cycle is complete, heat a griddle or heavy-based, non-stick frying pan over a medium heat. Brush the griddle or pan with the oil. Spoon single tablespoons of the batter onto the griddle and cook for a couple of minutes on each side until golden brown. Serve immediately or leave to cool on a wire rack and serve later, toasted.

bara brith

Bara Brith is Wales' most popular native bread. Bara Brith means 'speckled bread'; a description of this delicious loaf's interior, that is dotted with dried fruit. This rich and sweet dense bread would have traditionally been baked in the wall oven alongside the week's loaves, and is best served sliced and spread with Welsh butter.

you need

225 ml/8 fl oz/1 cup semi-skimmed milk
4 tbsp melted butter
1 large egg, beaten
1½ tsp salt
4 tbsp soft light brown sugar
50 g/2 oz/¼ cup mixed chopped peel
1½tsp mixed spice
450 g/16 oz/3 cups very strong white bread flour
1½ tsp instant or fast-acting dried yeast
75 g/3 oz/½ cup raisins
75 g/3 oz/½ cup currants
For the glaze:
1 egg
1 tbsp water
pinch of salt

to make

Pour the milk, butter and egg into the breadmaker bucket, followed by the salt, sugar, peel and spice. Cover the mixture with the flour and sprinkle the yeast over the top. Fit the bucket into the breadmaker and set to the basic white programme. Add the raisins and currants according to your manual's instructions, usually at the beginning of the second kneading cycle or when the machine bleeps. To make the glaze, whisk together the egg, water and salt. Forty-five minutes before the end of the cycle, carefully lift the lid and quickly brush the loaf with the glaze. When cooked, carefully shake the loaf from the bucket and stand it the right way up on a wire cooling rack. Leave for at least an hour before slicing and/or removing the paddle if necessary.

shearing cake

This light and fragrant cake, flavoured with caraway, nutmeg and lemon, was traditionally made at harvest time and its name is evidence of the popularity of sheep farming in Wales.

you need

125 g/4 oz/1/2 cup very soft butter
150 ml/5 fl oz/5/8 cup full cream milk
1 medium egg, beaten
pinch of salt
175 g/6 oz/13/16 cup caster sugar
zest of 1 lemon
2 tsp caraway seeds
pinch of ground nutmeg
225 g/8 oz/1 1/2 cups plain flour
1 tsp baking powder

to make

Put the butter, milk, egg, salt and sugar into the breadmaker bucket. Add the lemon zest, caraway seeds and nutmeg. Cover the mixture with the flour and baking powder. Fit the bucket into the breadmaker and set to the cake programme. After 5 minutes of the mixing cycle, scrape down the mixture on the sides of the bucket with a plastic spatula to ensure all the ingredients are evenly mixed. When cooked, remove the bucket from the machine and leave to cool for 5 minutes. Carefully shake the loaf from the bucket and stand it the right way up on a wire cooling rack. Leave to cool.

bara planc (bakestone bread)

This recipe is typical of the kind of quick, simple bread that, traditionally, was baked on a stone, iron or hot slate over, or in front of, the open fire. Thanks to the breadmaker's perfect baking environment and superior modern flour, this bread is likely to be a good deal lighter than its ancestor, but will still give you the flavour of days gone by.

This simple loaf relies on bicarbonate of soda as a raising agent and so will produce a close textured, dense bread more reminiscent of soda bread than a modern day yeast leavened loaf.

Wholesome and tasty, it's great served with a good cheddar cheese.

you need

300 ml/11 fl oz/1⅜ cup buttermilk
pinch of salt
1 tsp bicarbonate of soda
400 g/14 oz/2¾ cups strong white bread flour

to make

Pour the buttermilk into the breadmaker bucket, followed by the salt and bicarbonate of soda. Cover the mixture with the flour. Fit the bucket into the breadmaker and set to the cake programme. After 5 minutes of the mixing cycle, scrape down the mixture on the sides of the bucket with a plastic spatula to ensure all the ingredients are evenly mixed. When cooked, carefully shake the loaf from the bucket and stand it the right way up on a wire cooling rack. Leave to cool.

buttermilk in breadmaking

Natural buttermilk is the liquid left behind when cream has been churned and the fat removed as butter. When most rural households had their own cow or at least access to fresh milk and cream from a neighbouring farm, home butter production was the norm and, leaving nothing to waste, thrifty housewives used the 'waste' buttermilk to enrich their bread. Nowadays, we have to rely on commercially produced cultured buttermilk for our cooking. It's widely available in supermarkets.

oatbran and buttermilk bread

Oats and buttermilk were staple ingredients for many bakestone breads; evidence that oats were the most prevalent cereal crop grown in Wales, and that the region was also a great producer of butter. The pastoral country of south Wales has always supported dairy herds and even in the north some hardier breeds graze on the lower slopes of the uplands. Hereford and Welsh Black cattle were common here. They are stocky beef cattle and also provide a good yield of milk.

Curiously in Wales, the size of a dairy herd was a status symbol among farmers, so only the smallest possible numbers of animals were killed for meat. As herds grew so did the milk. Consequently, dairy products were plentiful and there was often a surplus. Farmers would add copious amounts of salt to butter to help preserve it, which is why Wales is famous for its distinctive rich, salty butter.

The by-product of the butter making process, buttermilk (see above), here combines beautifully with oatmeal to produce a light, rich and wholesome bread perfect for daily use.

you need

250 ml/9 fl oz/1⅛ cups buttermilk
1 medium egg, beaten
2 tbsp melted butter
1 tbsp runny Welsh honey
1 tsp salt
125 g/4 oz/1 cup oatbran
70g/21/2 oz/½ cup strong wholemeal bread flour
225g/8 oz/1½ cups very strong white bread flour
1½ tsp instant or fast-acting dried yeast

to make

Pour the buttermilk into the breadmaker bucket, followed by the egg, butter and honey. Add the salt and oatbran and cover the mixture with the flour. Finally, sprinkle the yeast over the top. Fit the bucket into the breadmaker and set to the basic white programme. Once cooked, carefully shake the loaf from the bucket and stand it the right way up on a wire cooling rack. Leave the bread to cool for at least an hour before slicing and/or removing the paddle if necessary.

caerphilly cheese bread with leek

This is a fantastic recipe, combining two of Wales' most popular ingredients – Caerphilly Cheese and the national emblem, leeks.

Caerphilly is famous for its cheese and its castle; in fact its notable history began when the Romans built an auxiliary fort there in AD 75. It is said the Christian missionary Saint Cenydd established a monastic site at Caerphilly that he later entrusted to his son Ffili. It is from this story and its Roman history that Caerphilly gets its name – the fort (caer) and Ffili.

Caerphilly cheese is mild and crumbly and was originally known as the 'miner's cheese' as it was a favoured by those working at the coalface. Historically Wales is renowned for cheese making and one of Shakespeare's characters said that he would rather trust a Welshman with his cheese than any other nationality! Today, farmhouse Caerphilly is still made in the traditional way by specialist dairies in Wales although the majority of commercial production is now carried out in the West Country. Caerphilly has a mild, slightly acidic taste that gives a subtle freshness to bread, and, when combined with the light onion tones of leek, it makes a really tasty loaf.

you need

75 g/3 oz/1 cup very finely chopped leek
3 tbsp melted butter
50 ml/2 fl oz/¼ cup soured cream
175 ml/6 fl oz/¾ cup water
1 tbsp granulated sugar
1½ tsp salt
¼ tsp finely ground black pepper
½ tsp dried mustard powder
50 g/2 oz/⅜ cup crumbled Caerphilly cheese
150 g/5¼ oz/1 cup strong wholemeal flour
300 g/11 oz/2 cups strong white bread flour
1½ tsp instant or fast-acting dried yeast

to make

Melt the butter in a saucepan, add the leek and cook over a gentle heat for 5 minutes. Pour the leek mixture into the breadmaker bucket, followed by the cream, water, sugar and salt. Add the pepper, mustard and cheese and cover the mixture with the flour. Finally, sprinkle the yeast over the top. Fit the bucket into the breadmaker and set to the basic white programme. Once cooked, carefully shake the loaf from the bucket and stand it the right way up on a wire cooling rack. Leave the bread to cool for at least an hour before slicing and/or removing the paddle if necessary.

teisen lap

I wasn't quite sure what to expect when I first baked a Teisen Lap, having never sampled it before, but it was a great surprise to find that this traditional Welsh fruit cake is pleasingly short and tasty. Its texture is unlike a standard British fruit cake having an interior more akin, I'd say, to that of a traditional rock cake. Offering something really different for tea time, it's delicious served sliced and buttered.

you need

350 g/12 oz/2¼ cups plain flour
75 g/3 oz/5⁄16 cup hard white vegetable fat
75 g/3 oz/5⁄16 cup butter
a little nutmeg
1½ tsp baking powder
75 g/3 oz/½ cup currants or raisins
3 large eggs, beaten
25 ml/1 fl oz/⅛ cup full cream milk

to make

Put the flour into a large bowl and rub in the fats until the mixture resembles fine breadcrumbs. Stir the nutmeg, baking powder and fruit into the flour mixture. Pour the eggs and milk into the breadmaker bucket and cover the liquid with the flour mixture. Fit the bucket into the breadmaker and set to the cake programme. After 5 minutes of the mixing cycle, scrape down the mixture on the sides of the bucket with a plastic spatula to ensure all the ingredients are evenly mixed. When cooked, remove the bucket from the machine and leave to cool for 5 minutes. Carefully shake the loaf from the bucket and stand it the right way up on a wire cooling rack. Leave to cool.

teisen fel (honey cake)

Beautifully moist and light, this sweet cake is also wonderfully rich and fragrant and is extremely quick to make using the breadmaker.

you need

225 g/8 oz/1½ cups plain flour
125 g/4 oz/½ cup butter
125 g/4 oz/⅜ cup Welsh honey
1 large egg, beaten
50ml/2 fl oz/¼ cup full cream milk
1 tsp ground cinnamon
125g/4 oz/¾ cup soft light brown sugar
½ tsp bicarbonate of soda

to make

Put the flour into a large bowl and rub in the fats until the mixture resembles fine breadcrumbs. Gently heat the honey in a saucepan until it flows freely from a spoon. Do not boil. Pour the egg and milk into the breadmaker bucket, followed by the warmed honey. Cover the liquid with the flour mixture. Finally, add the cinnamon, sugar and bicarbonate of soda. Fit the bucket into the breadmaker and set to the cake programme. After 5 minutes of the mixing cycle, scrape down the mixture on the sides of the bucket with a plastic spatula to ensure all the ingredients are evenly mixed. When cooked, remove the bucket from the machine and leave to cool for 5 minutes. Carefully shake the loaf from the bucket and stand it the right way up on a wire cooling rack.

honey, honey

Essentially, honey is the bee's store of winter food and is produced from the nectar that bees collect from flowers. Happily for us honey lovers, though, a good strong colony of bees will produce far more honey than is needed for survival, leaving a surplus which can be extracted from the comb in liquid form. Honey generally stays in this liquid form until it is extracted when it will slowly start to set and crystallize. Depending on the nectar varieties, some honeys will set more quickly than others. As British honey nearly always contains an element of raspberry or brassica, it tends to be of the quick setting variety.

There are around 30,000 beekeepers in Britain today, each offering a unique product with honey made from the nectar from the hive's locality. The colour and taste of honey differs according to where the bees gather their nectar and as bees can be kept almost anywhere, the choice of honey varieties is endless. Historically bees have been occupiers of orchards, smallholdings and farmland, feeding on the blossom of fruit trees, scented hedgerows, meadows and, of course, from our gardens.

welsh oatmeal pancakes

Served with bacon or simply with butter and honey, these traditional Welsh pancakes are perfect for breakfast or tea. Easy to make in the breadmaker, the bubbles in the yeast batter burst on cooking to produce light, lacy savoury pancakes that look wonderful and taste delicious.

Makes 10

you need

125 g/4 oz/7/8 cup fine oatmeal

1 medium egg, beaten

550 ml/20 fl oz/2 5/16 cups water

2 tbsp buttermilk

1 tsp salt

225 g/8 oz/1½ cups plain flour

2 tsp instant or fast-acting dried yeast

For the finish:

a little vegetable oil

to make

Soak the oatmeal in 550 ml/1 pint/2 5/16 cups of cold water overnight. The following day, strain the oatmeal and reserve the liquid. Put the soaked oatmeal into the breadmaker bucket, followed by the water, buttermilk and salt. Pour in 275 ml/10 fl oz/1¼ cups of the reserved liquid from the oatmeal. Cover the mixture with the flour and finally sprinkle the yeast over the top. Fit the bucket into the breadmaker and set to the dough programme. At the end of the cycle the batter should be frothy and well risen. Depending on your machine, it may be necessary to leave the batter in a warm place a little longer once the programme has finished until the batter is frothy and risen. Preheat the oven to 170°C/325°F/gas mark 3. Heat a griddle or heavy-bottomed frying pan over a medium heat. Brush the pan with the oil. Spoon a couple of tablespoons of the batter into the pan and let it spread to make a pancake about 17 cm/7 in across. Cook slowly until the pancake is full of tiny holes and firm enough to turn with a spatula. Turn the pancake and cook the other side. Transfer the pancake to the preheated oven to keep warm, if serving immediately. Repeat this process until all the batter is used.

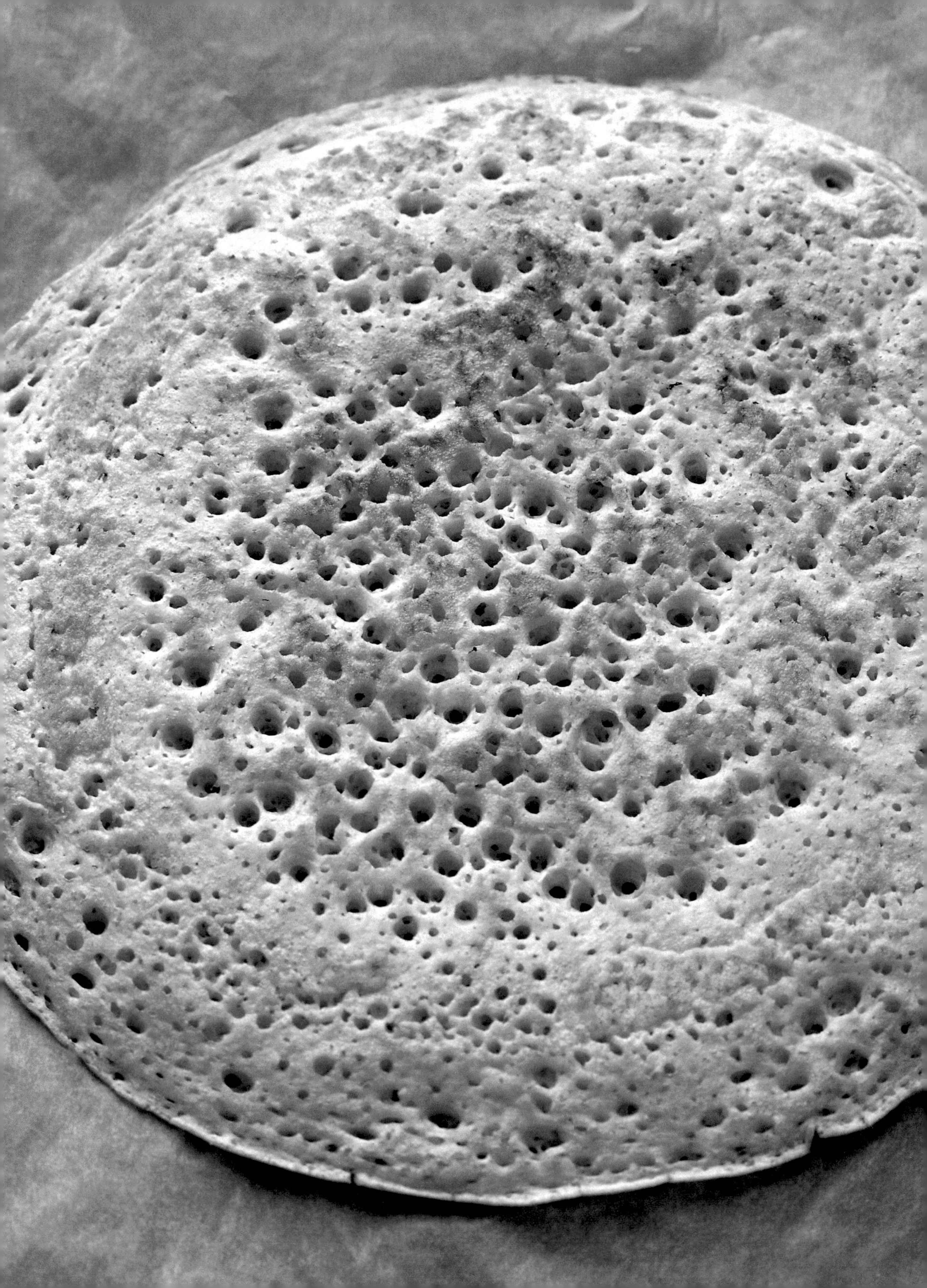

rye

Traditionally in Wales, as in other parts of the UK, bread baking was done once a week as this was the most time efficient way to ensure a well stocked larder. In addition to wheat and oats, Welsh housewives also made breads from barley, maslin (a mixture of flour that was made according to what was available) and often with rye.

Breadmakers cannot successfully produce a loaf made only from rye flour as its unfavourable gluten content produces a hard and dense bread. Far more pleasing, however, in terms of taste and texture, is bread made from rye flour blended with a good strong white wheat flour, as in the recipe below. With the distinctive tang of rye this wholesome loaf is light in texture with a rich and vibrant taste. For added variety, you might like to try adding a couple of tablespoons of caraway seeds which enhance the taste still further.

rye bread

you need

275 ml/10 fl oz/$1\frac{1}{4}$ cups water

2 tbsp granulated sugar

2 tsp salt

100 g/$3\frac{1}{2}$ oz/$\frac{3}{4}$ cup rye flour

350 g/12 oz/$2\frac{1}{4}$ cups very strong white bread flour

$1\frac{1}{2}$ tsp instant or fast-acting dried yeast

to make

Pour the water into the breadmaker bucket, followed by the sugar and salt. Cover the mixture with the flour and finally sprinkle the yeast over the top. Fit the bucket into the breadmaker and set to the basic white programme. Once cooked, carefully shake the loaf from the bucket and stand it the right way up on a wire cooling rack. Leave the bread to cool for at least an hour before slicing and/or removing the paddle if necessary.

rye bread with goat's cheese & thyme

I guarantee that the aroma of this bread cooking in your breadmaker will knock your socks off! The vibrancy of bread made with goat's cheese is wonderful; somehow the richness permeates every crumb and in my opinion the creamy, fragrant goat's cheese of Wales is our nation's best. Here, it's blended with tangy rye flour and sweet thyme to give a heavenly and extremely versatile bread which has long been a firm favourite of mine.

you need

225 ml/8 fl oz/1 cup water
2 tbsp sunflower oil
1 tbsp sugar
1 tsp salt
50 g/2 oz/3/8 cup diced Welsh goat's cheese
1 tsp fresh or dried thyme
70 g/2½ oz/½ cup rye flour
375 g/13 oz/2½ cups wholesome white very strong bread flour
1¼ tsp instant or fast-acting dried yeast

to make

Pour the water into the breadmaker bucket, followed by the oil, sugar and salt. Add the goat's cheese and thyme and cover the mixture with the flour. Finally, sprinkle the yeast over the top. Fit the bucket into the breadmaker and set to the basic white programme. Once cooked, carefully shake the loaf from the bucket and stand it the right way up on a wire cooling rack. Leave the bread to cool for at least an hour before slicing and/or removing the paddle if necessary.

welsh claypot bread

Pot breads originated from the method of baking breads over a peat fire in a cauldron-like iron pot. A string of dough would often be used to 'seal' the lid of the pot, encasing the loaf inside. Acting like a miniature oven, this sealed pot would protect the bread from the open fire and provide the even temperature required for baking. In more recent times, the quirky idea of baking in clay flowerpots in a regular oven has succeeded the cauldron and fire method. Clay pots radiate heat, making them perfect for baking bread and with their obvious visual appeal, this is an attractive and surprisingly simple way to bake rustic loaves.

I've given a complete breadmaker recipe here using dried onion and chives (as fresh onion can spoil breadmaker loaves if not used with care) and a selection of fresh native herbs. This versatile loaf is great with soup and stews and will make a delicious accompaniment to your favourite cheese.

If you'd like to try baking this in clay pots use the dough cycle and $2\frac{1}{2}$ tsp of yeast. Choose new, clean terracotta pots and brush them liberally inside and out with vegetable oil. Bake the pots in a hot oven while something else is cooking. If you repeat this process several times the pots will become almost non-stick and will make the perfect mould for baking bread. Don't forget to stand the pots the right way up as the bread proves to stop the dough coming out of the hole in the base.

you need

150 ml/5 fl oz/$\frac{5}{8}$ cup semi-skimmed milk
125 ml/4 fl oz/$\frac{1}{2}$ cup water
1 medium egg, beaten
4 tbsp melted butter
3 tbsp dried onion flakes
1 small clove of garlic, crushed
1 tbsp dried chopped chives
1 tbsp chopped fresh parsley
1 tsp chopped fresh sage
1 tbsp granulated sugar
$1\frac{1}{2}$ tsp salt
100 g/$3\frac{1}{2}$ oz/$\frac{3}{4}$ cup strong wholemeal bread flour
350 g/12 oz/$2\frac{1}{4}$ cups strong white bread flour

to make

Pour the milk and water into the breadmaker bucket, followed by the egg, butter, onion and garlic. Add the herbs, sugar and salt. Cover the mixture with the flour and finally sprinkle the yeast over the top. Fit the bucket into the breadmaker and set to the basic white programme. Once cooked, carefully shake the loaf from the bucket and stand it the right way up on a wire cooling rack. Leave the bread to cool for at least an hour before slicing and/or removing the paddle if necessary.

northern ireland

northern ireland

Across the Irish Sea lies our most westerly province – Northern Ireland. Separated from the south by Carlingford Lough in the east and the boundaries of Armagh, Dungannon and Fermanagh in the south, the region is perfectly placed to enjoy the bounty of both land and sea. It is said that in Ireland no person is more than three generations away from the land and it is perhaps for this reason that the food in the province reflects, so greatly, traditional country life. Influenced by coastline, climate and countryside, this region enjoys some of our greatest specialities.

With high rainfall and a temperate climate, grass grows well here. Where dairy cattle graze, rich milk is produced and from it comes a fantastic range of butter and cheese. For beef cattle the conditions are ideal as they can graze year round giving an added succulence to Irish beef which is used locally in dishes like Spiced Beef – a traditional Christmas speciality made by rubbing brisket with spices and leaving in a cool place for at least a week before slowly cooking with root vegetables and stout.

Freshwater lakes and rivers provide a rich menu of fish from salmon and trout to pike, perch and eel. Along the coastline shellfish, including the finest lobsters, mussels and oysters, are caught, while the sea provides cod, skate, herring and mackerel. From the sea also come two vegetable specialities: the red seaweed Dulse – often mixed with mashed potato to make Dulse Champ – and Carrageen – an Irish Moss that is eaten either fresh or dried.

Regional food remains on the daily menu in Ireland with dishes like the Ulster Fry – a feast of fried sausages, bacon, eggs, mushrooms, tomatoes, Farls (page 136) and Potato Bread (page 132) – served for breakfast. At last we mention potatoes or 'murphys' as they are called locally. The Irish make the most of this national treasure, using it in various soups, cakes, dumplings, scones, pies, pancakes and breads, like Boxty (opposite).

potatoes

It is uncertain how the potato first came to Ireland; some say Walter Raleigh introduced it and others say that it was simply washed ashore from the shipwrecks of the Spanish Armada that sunk off the Irish coast. Whatever its origins, the potato was soon the mainstay of the Irish diet. Farmers found that the humble tuber could produce far more food per acre than anything they had grown before and that it was a wholesome and versatile food, too.

boxty bread

'Boxty on the griddle, boxty in the pan,
The wee one in the middle is for Mary Ann.
Boxty on the griddle, boxty in the pan,
If you don't eat boxty, you'll never get your man.'

Boxty Bread is traditionally made from a mixture of cooked and grated raw potatoes mixed to a dough with flour and milk and baked on a griddle. For convenience the recipe below is made on a complete breadmaker (cake) cycle though the mix will cook on a griddle or in a heavy based frying pan equally well. Boxty Bread should be buttered and eaten fresh and hot. The Irish also use the same basic mix – thinned with milk – to make a kind of pancake that is eaten with brown sugar and butter. Both versions are popular at Halloween.

you need

150 ml/5 fl oz/⅝ cup full cream milk
3 tbsp butter
½ tsp salt
¼ tsp white pepper
250 g/9 oz/1¾ cups grated raw potatoes
350 g/12 oz/1½ cups warm mashed potato
150 g/5¼ oz/1 cup wholemeal self-raising flour
150 g/5¼ oz/1 cup self-raising flour
2 tsp baking powder

to make

Pour the milk and butter into the breadmaker bucket, followed by the salt, pepper and potatoes. Cover the mixture with the flour and baking powder. Fit the bucket into the breadmaker and set to the cake or scone programme. If you have an adjustable crust facility on your machine, select the dark setting. After 5 minutes of the mixing cycle, scrape down the sides of the bucket with a plastic spatula to ensure all the ingredients are evenly mixed. When cooked, remove the bucket from the machine and leave to cool for 5 minutes. Carefully shake the loaf from the bucket and stand it the right way up on a wire cooling rack. Leave to cool.

potato bread

Here is a quick and easy version of this Irish classic made especially for breadmakers. This moist, wholesome loaf offers a pleasing full flavour making it perfect for any occasion. The Irish, however, like to serve this for breakfast and I have to confess that when I tested this, my husband used it the next day to make fried bread, and it was utterly delicious.

you need

125 ml/4 fl oz/½ cup full cream milk
125 ml/4 fl oz/½ cup water
2 tsp salt
2 tsp granulated sugar
125 g/4 oz/¾ cup warm mashed potato
450 g/16 oz/3 cups strong white bread flour
1¼ tsp instant or fast-acting dried yeast

to make

Pour the milk and water into the breadmaker bucket, followed by the salt and sugar. Add the mashed potato and cover the mixture with the flour. Finally sprinkle the yeast over the top. Fit the bucket into the breadmaker and set to the basic white programme. Once cooked, carefully shake the loaf from the bucket and stand it the right way up on a wire cooling rack. Leave the bread to cool for at least an hour before slicing and/or removing the paddle if necessary.

potato and bacon bread

Northern Ireland produces much of the UK's bacon and there are traditional local cures to be found like the Ulster Roll. The salty flavour of bacon goes so well with potatoes and is a classic combination in many traditional Irish dishes, including the Ulster Fry breakfast. In fact, many old Irish potato breads were cooked in bacon fat. So, I decided to try the combination in bread dough and found that the resulting loaf was wholesome, moist and tasty with a just a hint of smokiness from the bacon. This is great bread for bacon sandwiches and also fantastic when served with eggs – try it for yourself.

you need

4 rashers smoked back bacon
125 ml/4 fl oz/½ cup full cream milk
125 ml/4 fl oz/½ cup water
2 tbsp melted butter
200 g/7 oz/1 cup warm mashed potato
¼ tsp finely ground white pepper
1½ tsp salt
¼ tsp cumin powder
1 tbsp granulated sugar
70 g/2½ oz/½ cup rye flour
150 g/5¼ oz/1 cup strong brown flour
225 g/8 oz/1½ cups strong white bread flour

to make

Fry or grill the bacon, dice and leave to cool. Pour the milk and water into the breadmaker bucket, followed by the butter and mashed potato. Add the pepper, salt, cumin, sugar and the cooled bacon. Cover the mixture with the flour and sprinkle the yeast over the top. Fit the bucket into the breadmaker and set to the basic white programme. Once cooked, carefully shake the loaf from the bucket and stand it the right way up on a wire cooling rack. Leave the bread to cool for at least an hour before slicing and/or removing the paddle if necessary.

yellowmeal bread

Yellowmeal is the bright yellow meal made from maize. Irish history first recalls maize meal (cornmeal) being used in bread in the 19th century. This versatile traditional loaf has a rich, yellow colour and a distinctive grainy texture.

you need

1 medium egg, beaten
275 ml/10 fl oz/1¼ cups water
3 tbsp melted butter
1 tbsp granulated sugar
1½ tsp salt
150 g/5¼ oz/1 cup fine cornmeal
150 g/5¼ oz/1 cup wholesome white very strong bread flour
225 g/8 oz/1½ cups very strong white bread flour
1½ tsp instant or fast-acting dried yeast

to make

Pour the egg and water into the breadmaker bucket, followed by the butter, sugar and salt. Cover the mixture with the cornmeal and flour and finally sprinkle the yeast over the top. Fit the bucket into the breadmaker and set to the basic white programme. Once cooked, carefully shake the loaf from the bucket and stand it the right way up on a wire cooling rack. Leave the bread to cool for at least an hour before slicing and/or removing the paddle if necessary.

farls

The word farl means 'fourth part' and farls are in fact quarter circles in shape. Traditionally made with wheat flour and sometimes with potatoes and oats, the farl dough is shaped into a round and either cut into quarters completely or marked almost through so that the bread can be easily divided once cooked. As with most traditional Irish breads, farls were usually baked on a stone over a peat fire. They can be baked in a conventional oven, as shown in the picture, if finished shape is not a priority, the breadmaker can do the whole job for you as in the recipe below.

As farls depend on the chemical reaction between the acidic buttermilk and bicarbonate of soda to rise, expect a dense bread reminiscent of soda bread. Farls are best eaten very fresh and are delicious served with a hearty stew or as part of a traditional fried breakfast.

you need

350 ml/12 fl oz/1½ cups buttermilk
¾ tsp salt
¾ tsp granulated sugar
225 g/8 oz/1½ cups plain flour
225 g/8 oz/1½cups plain wholemeal flour

to make

Pour the buttermilk into the breadmaker bucket, followed by the salt and sugar. Cover the mixture with the flour and finally sprinkle the bicarbonate of soda over. Fit the bucket into the breadmaker and set to the cake programme. Lift the lid of the breadmaker a couple of times during the first mixing, to ensure that all of the ingredients are thoroughly incorporated into the dough. If necessary, scrape down the sides of the bucket with a plastic spatula to ensure all the ingredients are evenly mixed. If the mixture looks a little dry, add a little more buttermilk. When cooked, carefully shake the loaf from the bucket and stand it the right way up on a wire cooling rack. Leave the bread to cool for at least an hour before slicing and/or removing the paddle if necessary.

soda bread

Soda bread is the classic of all Irish breads and has many variations that, like farls, were originally cooked on a griddle over an Irish peat fire. Today, these traditional recipes can be easily baked in conventional ovens. As classic Irish soda bread requires quick mixing and the lightest of handling, it's not best suited to the breadmaker but is easily made by hand. If you like, you can then bake it in the breadmaker using the 'bake' cycle to save heating the oven.

For a simple soda bread sieve together 450 g/16 oz/3 cups of plain flour, 1 tsp of salt and 1 tsp of bicarbonate of soda. Make a well in the centre and pour in 425 ml/15 fl oz/$1\frac{7}{8}$ cups of buttermilk. Mix to a soft dough adding a little more buttermilk if necessary. The secret is to not over mix the dough, so be quick. Shape into a round and cut a cross in the centre. Then prick the four triangles (made by cutting the top of the loaf with a knife), as Irish folklore says this lets the fairies out! Then bake in a preheated oven at 200°C/400°F/gas mark 6 for about 25 minutes. Alternatively, place the shaped loaf into the breadmaker bucket and cook using the 'bake' cycle.

soda bread with raisins

This isn't really a true soda bread as it is leavened with yeast, but because of this it cooks well in the breadmaker.

you need

1 large egg, beaten
250 ml/9 fl oz/$1\frac{1}{8}$ cups buttermilk
1 tsp melted butter
75 g/3 oz/$\frac{5}{16}$ cup granulated sugar
1 tsp salt
100 g/$3\frac{1}{2}$ oz/$\frac{5}{8}$ cup raisins
150 g/$5\frac{1}{4}$ oz/1 cup strong brown flour
300 g/11 oz/2 cups strong white bread flour
$1\frac{1}{2}$ tsp instant or fast-acting dried yeast
1 tsp baking powder

to make

Pour the egg, buttermilk and butter into the breadmaker bucket, followed by the sugar, salt and raisins. Cover the mixture with the flour and sprinkle the yeast and baking powder over the top. Fit the bucket into the breadmaker and set to the quick bread or turbo programme*. Once cooked, carefully shake the loaf from the bucket and stand it the right way up on a wire cooling rack. Leave the bread to cool for at least an hour before slicing and/or removing the paddle if necessary.

*Consult your manual for the best programme for your breadmaker. A programme with a single kneading and rising cycle is required. Sometimes this is also referred to as the rapid, quick bread or gluten-free programme.

treacle soda bread

Sweet and dense, this delicious bread will make a refreshing change to cakes on the tea table. It's delicious served buttered.

you need

350 ml/11 fl oz/1 3/8 cups buttermilk
2 tsp black treacle
1/2 tsp salt
1 tbsp sugar
450 g/16 oz/3 cups plain flour
1 tsp bicarbonate of soda

to make

Put the buttermilk and treacle into a saucepan and gently heat until the treacle is incorporated, stirring continuously. Do not boil. Put the warm mixture into the breadmaker bucket and add the salt and sugar. Cover the mixture with the flour and finally sprinkle the bicarbonate of soda over the top. Fit the bucket into the breadmaker and set to the cake, quick bread or turbo programme.* Once cooked, carefully shake the loaf from the bucket and stand it the right way up on a wire cooling rack. Leave the bread to cool for at least an hour before slicing and/or removing the paddle if necessary.

*Consult your manual for the best programme for your breadmaker. A programme with a single kneading and rising cycle is required. Sometimes this is also referred to as the rapid, quick bread or gluten-free programme.

treacle

Treacle is the generic name for any syrup made from the refining of sugar cane, so the term covers Golden Syrup, Black Treacle and Molasses. However, strictly speaking, molasses differs from treacle in that it is obtained from the drainings of raw sugar while treacle comes from the syrup made from the sugar itself.

Golden syrup has a clear golden colour and a sweet, rich, buttery flavour. It's used as a spread, a topping and also in recipes for tarts, puddings and cakes. By contrast the viscous, dark black treacle tastes of burnt caramel and gives a much stronger flavour, making it a common ingredient in confectionery, baked goods (like bread and fruit cakes), glazes, sauces and stews.

quick sour bread

We all love short cuts in the kitchen, especially when the results are good. So here's a recipe that will give a flavour reminiscent of a slowly proved sourdough bread without the preparation time.

Soured milk and cream are no strangers to Irish cuisine as records show that the Irish have been known for liking a drink of sour milk. Records of the various stages of souring with apt descriptions of the taste and texture were recorded in the 11th century leading us to believe that the Irish were actually connoisseurs of sour milk drinking. The milk would be termed 'very thick milk, a milk not too thick, a milk of long thickness, a milk of medium thickness and of yellow bubbling milk, the swallowing of which needs chewing'.

Thankfully, soured cream provides this flavour for us in a much more appetising way and is the base of the distinctive flavour in this light and airy bread.

you need

125ml/4 fl oz/½ cup soured cream
125ml/4 fl oz/½ cup water
1 medium egg, beaten
2 tsp cider vinegar
1½ tsp salt
1 tbsp granulated sugar
450g/16 oz/3 cups strong white bread flour
1¼ tsp instant or fast-acting dried yeast
For the glaze:
1 egg
1 tbsp water
pinch of salt
poppy seeds

to make

Pour the cream and water into the breadmaker bucket, followed by the egg, vinegar, salt and sugar. Cover the mixture with the flour and finally sprinkle the yeast over the top. Fit the bucket into the breadmaker and set to the basic white programme. To make the glaze, whisk together the egg, water and salt. Forty-five minutes before the end of the cycle, carefully lift the lid and quickly brush the loaf with the glaze and sprinkle over the poppy seeds. When cooked, carefully shake the loaf from the bucket and stand it the right way up on a wire cooling rack. Leave for at least an hour before slicing and/or removing the paddle if necessary.

brown oatmeal bread

In the early days in Northern Ireland, oats were ground by hand (between two stones) or in a rotary quern (a mechanized stone grinder). In this contraption, grain was poured in from the top and on its way through the machine was ground between stones to fall away as a coarsely ground meal.

Oatbran is a modern-day equivalent of coarse oatmeal, with the added goodness of wheat bran, and can be found with the breakfast cereals in most supermarkets and health food shops. It adds a wonderfully clean, nutty flavour to bread and gives a rustic texture to this interpretation of a traditional oat-laden loaf.

you need

275 ml/10 fl oz/1¼ cups water
3 tbsp soured cream
1 tbsp granulated sugar
1½ tsp salt
100 g/3½ oz/¾ cup oatbran
400 g/14 oz/2¾ cups strong brown bread flour
1½ tsp instant or fast-acting dried yeast

to make

Pour the water into the breadmaker bucket, followed by the cream, sugar and salt. Cover the mixture with the oatbran and flour and finally sprinkle the yeast over the top. Fit the bucket into the breadmaker and set to the basic white programme. Once cooked, carefully shake the loaf from the bucket and stand it the right way up on a wire cooling rack. Leave the bread to cool for at least an hour before slicing and/or removing the paddle if necessary.

porter cake

This dark, rich fruit cake from Northern Ireland uses porter. Porter is a weaker variety of stout, traditionally the working man's pint, that was drunk to take the worries away from the day. Known as 'plain' to the locals, one Irishman's poem reads:

When things go wrong and will not come right,
Though you do the best you can,
When life looks black as the hour of night,
A pint of plain is your only man.

Porter can be hard to find today. Its name has almost become an interchangeable term for Irish stout that, incidentally, works equally well if used in this recipe.

you need

2 large eggs, beaten
150 ml/5 fl oz/$^{5}/_{8}$ cup stout or porter
finely grated zest of 1 lemon
1 tsp mixed spice
100 g/3$^{1}/_{2}$ oz/$^{5}/_{8}$ cup soft light brown sugar
100 g/3$^{1}/_{2}$ oz/$^{7}/_{16}$ cup very soft butter
275 g/10 oz/1$^{3}/_{4}$ cups mixed dried fruit
225 g/8 oz/1$^{1}/_{2}$ cups self-raising flour

to make

Pour the eggs and stout into the breadmaker bucket, followed by the lemon, spice, sugar and butter. Cover the mixture with the fruit, flour and baking powder. Fit the bucket into the breadmaker and set to the cake programme. Lift the lid of the breadmaker a couple of times during the first mixing, to ensure that all of the ingredients are thoroughly incorporated into the dough. If necessary, scrape down the mixture on the sides of the bucket with a plastic spatula to ensure all the ingredients are evenly mixed. When cooked, remove the bucket from the machine and leave to cool for 5 minutes. Carefully shake the loaf from the bucket and stand it the right way up on a wire cooling rack. Leave to cool.

barm brack

Barm Brack is the classic Irish yeasted fruit bread and is most frequently served at Halloween. Traditionally it was baked in a 'bastable oven' – a three-legged cauldron with a lid that was suspended on chains over a peat fire. After the bread was put in the pot the lid was covered with pieces of smoldering peat to help ensure even cooking of the loaf.

This rich fruit bread is fragranced with caraway and often sweetened with currants giving it an added dimension over other regional fruit breads. Serve simply sliced and buttered, ideally with a good pot of tea.

you need

2 medium eggs, beaten
200 ml/7 fl oz/$^{7}/_{8}$ cup water
6 tbsp melted butter
1$^{1}/_{2}$ tsp salt
5 tbsp granulated sugar
4 tsp caraway seeds
450 g/16 oz/3 cups very strong white bread flour
1$^{1}/_{2}$tsp instant or fast-acting dried yeast
75 g/3 oz/$^{1}/_{2}$ cup currants (optional)

to make

Pour the eggs, water and butter into the breadmaker bucket, followed by the salt, sugar and caraway seeds. Cover the mixture with the flour and sprinkle the yeast over the top. Fit the bucket into the breadmaker and set to the basic white programme. Add the currants, if desired, according to your manual's instructions, usually at the beginning of the second kneading cycle, or when the machine bleeps. Once cooked, carefully shake the loaf from the bucket and stand it the right way up on a wire cooling rack. Leave the bread to cool for at least an hour before slicing and/or removing the paddle if necessary.

scotland

scotland

Between the tip of Orkney in the Atlantic Ocean and the Borders lies beautiful Scotland – a land of mountains, hills, lochs and glens. This is a region of contrasts: it's home to the vibrant cities of Glasgow and Edinburgh and also still, in places, home to the tenant farmers working a small patch of land under the traditional crofting system.

The rugged terrain makes Scotland one of the country's premier locations for shooting grouse, partridge, pheasant, wild duck and deer. Fishing for trout and salmon in the lochs and rivers is popular with tourists and locals alike. Whisky, too, attracts visitors from afar, with distilleries situated on both the mainland and islands. Alongside the staples of meat and fish, Scotland also holds its own in fruit and vegetable production, growing both tough crops like turnips, peas and potatoes and soft fruits like raspberries, tayberries and gooseberries.

Crofting here has a harsh history: it was a difficult life with functional, sustaining foods being the mainstays of the diet. The barrel of oats or girnel (as it was known) would have contained the essential ingredients for oatcakes and bannocks, and provided the perfect agent for thickening soups, coating meat and fish, and for making basic dishes like skirlie – a mix of beef, suet, onion and oatmeal fried together in a pan. Classic Scottish recipes, like the Haggis, ensured nothing was wasted. Traditionally made with offal and off-cuts of meat that in better times would have been discarded, Haggis is still enjoyed today – not only on Burn's night – but year round as Scotland's national dish.

Baking is an important tradition in Scotland and no breakfast would be complete without the flour-dusted Scottish Morning Loaf (page 150) served warm from the oven. Tea time sees some of the most famous Scottish bakes from Dundee cake (page 153) to Gingerbread (page 152). And then there's always time in the evening for a wee dram of the world renowned Scotch whisky.

parkin

This classic combination of oatmeal and treacle is popular throughout Northern England and Scotland. Hearty and sustaining, it's typical of traditional, hard working food that acts as a functional treat – making it no surprise that Parkin actually improves with age rather than going stale like most traditional cakes.

Parkin is a great recipe for the breadmaker which effortlessly turns out this sweetly spiced, dense and grainy cake. Once cooked, Parkin benefits from being kept in an airtight container for a good few days before eating, during which time it matures and softens, becoming a real pleasure to eat.

you need

100 ml/3½ fl oz/¼ cup black treacle
100 ml/3½ fl oz/¼ cup golden syrup
50 ml/2 fl oz/¼ cup melted butter
½ tsp bicarbonate of soda
150 ml/5 fl oz/⅝ cup full cream milk
1 medium egg, beaten
175 g/6 oz/1⅛ cups medium oatmeal
½ tsp salt
25 g/1 oz/1/16 cup granulated sugar
½ tsp ground ginger
225 g/8 oz/1½ cups plain flour

to make

Put the treacle and syrup into a saucepan and gently heat until it runs freely from a spoon. Do not boil. Pour the treacle and syrup into the breadmaker bucket, followed by the melted butter. Stir the bicarbonate of soda into the milk and pour this mixture into the bucket, followed by the beaten egg. Cover the mixture with the oatmeal, salt, sugar, ginger and finally the flour. Fit the bucket into the breadmaker and set to the cake programme. Once cooked, carefully shake the Parkin from the bucket and stand it the right way up on a wire cooling rack. Leave to cool for at least an hour before slicing and/or removing the paddle if necessary. Parkin is best stored in an airtight tin for up to a week before eating.

scottish morning loaf/rolls

What breakfast would be complete without the traditional soft Scottish Morning Loaf served warm with butter and heather honey or Dundee marmalade?

Enriched with full cream milk this light, airy bread has no additional fat, so it is best served fresh and eaten warm on the day it is made. This bread is traditionally dusted with flour before baking, but I like to add variety and sometimes glaze with egg to give an alternative texture. If you are making rolls you can dust half with flour and glaze the other half.

Makes 1 loaf or 8 rolls

you need

150 ml/5 fl oz/⅝ cup full cream milk

150 ml/5 fl oz/⅝ cup water

1 tbsp granulated sugar

1½ tsp salt

450 g/16 oz/3 cups very strong white bread flour

2½ tsp instant or fast-acting dried yeast*

For the finish and the glaze:

flour

or

1 egg

1 tbsp water

pinch of salt

to make

Lightly grease a baking sheet. Pour the milk and water into the breadmaker bucket, followed by the sugar and salt. Cover the mixture with the flour and finally sprinkle the yeast over the top. Fit the bucket into the breadmaker and set to the dough programme. When the cycle is complete, turn the dough out on to a lightly floured surface and knead until smooth. Divide the dough into 8 equally sized pieces. Shape each piece into a ball and then flatten until about 2.5cm/1 in thick. Put the rolls on to the baking sheet. Cover with a tea towel and leave in a warm place to prove until doubled in size. Either dust generously with flour or brush with the egg glaze. To make the glaze, whisk together the egg, water and salt. Bake in a preheated oven at 200°C/400°F/gas mark 6 for 15–20 minutes.

*If you would like to make this recipe as a loaf (as shown in picture opposite), use the basic white programme and reduce the yeast to 1¼ tsp.

sweet bakes for tea

Scotland is renowned for baking and, as in the North of England, since Victorian times, high tea is often served as the main meal of the day at around five or six o'clock. The meal often comprises savouries like fish and chips, kippers, haddock or beef 'ham pies' followed by any one of Scotland's famous cakes. Many of these traditional tea-time recipes can be effectively reproduced using a breadmaker and below are some of my favourites.

edinburgh gingerbread

Edinburgh's version of gingerbread is different again in both taste and texture to that made in other regions of the country (alternatives on pages 82 and 102). With the addition of sultanas and almonds, this extra-rich version is a real treat. As with most dense cakes, it benefits from a few days in an airtight container before eating as allowing the cake to mature and soften makes it even better to eat.

you need

175 g/6 oz/$^{13}/_{16}$ cup butter
175 g/6 oz/$^{1}/_{2}$ cup black treacle
125 g/4 oz/$^{3}/_{4}$ cup soft light brown sugar
6 tbsp milk
2 medium eggs, beaten
225 g/8 oz/1$^{1}/_{2}$ cups plain flour
1 tsp bicarbonate of soda
2 tsp ground ginger
1 tsp ground cinnamon
pinch of salt
50 g/2 oz/$^{1}/_{4}$ cup sultanas
50 g/2 oz/$^{1}/_{2}$ cup flaked almonds

to make

Put the butter, treacle and sugar into a saucepan and gently heat until everything has melted and amalgamated together. Do not boil. Pour into the breadmaker bucket, followed by the milk and eggs. Cover the mixture with the flour and add the bicarbonate of soda, ginger, cinnamon and salt. Finally, add the sultanas and almonds. Fit the bucket into the breadmaker and set to the cake programme. After 5 minutes of the mixing cycle, scrape down the mixture on the sides of the bucket with a plastic spatula to ensure all the ingredients are evenly mixed. When cooked, remove the bucket from the machine and leave to cool for 5 minutes. Carefully shake the loaf from the bucket and stand it the right way up on a wire cooling rack. Leave to cool.

dundee cake

Almond topped Dundee Cake has to be the best known of all Scottish bakes – light, sweet and fruity, it is traditionally topped with almonds. It is named after the town of Dundee where it originates – a place also famous for marmalade. Some say marmalade used to feature in the recipe but I could find no record of this.

you need

250 g/9 oz/1 1/8 cups soft butter
4 large eggs, beaten
grated rind of 1 lemon
grated rind of 1 orange
225 g/8 oz/1 1/2 cups light soft brown sugar
250g/9 oz/1 3/4 cups plain flour
2 tsp baking powder
125g/4 oz/1 cup mixed dried fruit
25g/1 oz/1/4 cup ground almonds
For the finish:
1 tbsp flaked almonds

to make

Put all the ingredients into the breadmaker bucket in the order given above. Fit the bucket into the breadmaker and set to the cake programme. After a few minutes of the first mixing, lift the lid of the breadmaker and scrape down the sides of the bucket with a plastic spatula to ensure all the ingredients are evenly mixed. Once the mixing part of the cycle has finished, sprinkle over the flaked almonds. When the cycle is complete, remove the bucket from the machine and leave the cake to cool for 5 minutes. Carefully shake the cake from the bucket and stand it the right way up on a wire cooling rack. Leave to cool.

dundee marmalade

It was in the 1700s that a storm-bound ship first docked in Dundee harbour with its curious cargo of Seville sours – the incredibly bitter oranges. At this time the town did not normally trade with Spain and so locals found the cargo especially fascinating. It is said that John Keiller came across the fruit on his walk to the harbour and took some home to his wife who ran a bakery business. She was an inventive cook and transformed the bitter fruit into a delicious new conserve. Today, nearly 300 years later, Dundee Orange Marmalade is still enjoyed the world over.

aberdeen butteries

Also known as Rowies, these layered crispy delicacies are not unlike croissants though they are round in shape. They are really just flaky pastry circles and have a light, layered appearance and rich, buttery taste. I think that they are best served with whipped cream and jam.

Makes 12–15

you need

300 ml/11 fl oz/1^3/$_8$ cups water

^{1}/$_2$ tsp salt

1 tbsp caster sugar

450 g/16 oz/3 cups plain flour

2^1/$_2$ tsp instant or fast-acting dried yeast

225 g/8 oz/1 cup butter (at room temperature)

100 g/3^1/$_2$ oz/^{7}/$_{16}$ cup hard white vegetable fat (at room temperature)

to make

Lightly grease a baking tray. Pour the water into the breadmaker bucket, followed by the salt and sugar. Cover the mixture with the flour and sprinkle the yeast over the top. Fit the bucket into the breadmaker and set to the dough programme. Mix the two fats together on a plate and divide into three (as equally as possible). When the dough cycle is complete, turn the dough out onto a lightly floured surface and knead until smooth. This is a sticky dough, so take care not to add too much flour and dry it out. Roll the dough into a long strip and spread a third of the fat into the centre third of the dough. Fold the dough over the fat from the top and bottom like an envelope. Turn the dough 45 degrees and then roll out as before. Repeat this process until all the fat has been added. If any fat comes to the surface making it sticky, sprinkle a little flour over it. Once all the fat is added, roll and fold twice more. Finally, roll the dough out to a thickness of about 2.5cm/1 in and use a plain cutter to cut out 12–15 rounds from it. If you have to re-roll the dough, take care to stack the pieces to ensure the layers created by the rolling and folding remain horizontal. Place the buns on to the baking sheet, cover with a tea towel and leave in a warm place to prove until doubled in size. Bake in a preheated oven at 200°C/400°F/gas mark 6 for 20 minutes until golden brown and puffy.

raspberry ripple buns

I wanted to include a recipe using fresh raspberries in this chapter, in celebration of Scotland's production of this classic British fruit. I had in my mind a light and airy dough rippled with fresh raspberry pieces. After many trials I found that using raspberry coulis actually gave better results as it happily wound its way through the dough giving the rippled effect I was trying to achieve inside light and buttery buns.

These buns are equally delicious made with other traditional Scottish fruits like tayberries, loganberries, blackcurrants or gooseberries. Simply make your own coulis by blitzing the fruit in a blender and sieving out any pips. Cook hard fruits like gooseberries and blackcurrants in sugar syrup first (see page 60 for instructions).

Makes 12

you need

250 ml/9 fl oz/1⅛ cups water
1 medium egg, beaten
1 tbsp melted butter
2 tbsp raspberry jam (without pips)
1 tsp salt
450 g/16 oz/3 cups very strong white bread flour
2½ tsp instant or fast-acting dried yeast
50 ml/2 fl oz/⅛ cup raspberry coulis

For the glaze:
melted butter

to make

Lightly grease a large muffin tin. Pour the water into the breadmaker bucket, followed by the egg, butter, jam and salt. Cover the mixture with the flour and sprinkle the yeast over the top. Fit the bucket into the breadmaker and set to the dough programme. When the cycle is complete, turn the dough out on to a lightly floured surface and divide into 12 equally-sized pieces. Press each piece of dough into a flat circle and make an indentation in the centre of each circle. Put a teaspoon of coulis into the centre of each piece of dough. Bring the edges of each bun up and press together firmly to seal. As this is quite a light dough, this can be quite a sticky job. Don't be too fussy – if some of the coulis leaks out, don't worry, just concentrate on getting the top edges sealed together. Try not to dry the dough out by adding too much flour. Place each bun into the tin with the joined side uppermost. Cover with a damp tea towel and leave in a warm place to prove for 30 minutes. Brush with half of the melted butter and bake in a preheated oven at 220°C/425°F/gas mark 7 for 12–14 minutes, until puffy and golden. While hot, brush again with the rest of the melted butter and transfer to a wire cooling rack. Leave to cool.

berries

The Scottish argue that their berries are the best in the country with a sweetness and concentration of flavour that comes from the slow ripening conditions of a cooler climate. Whatever your opinion British (and Scottish) berries are great ingredients, served on their own or in desserts, cakes, jams, tarts or breads.

Late June to September is the season for soft fruit and the more unusual varieties include loganberries – a cross between a raspberry and the American dewberry. Larger, darker and softer than raspberries, they have a sharp flavour and so you may need a little extra sugar when cooking with them. They are generally in season from June to August.

Tayberries have a shorter season – between early July and mid-August – and are a cross between a blackberry and a raspberry. Large and conical in shape, they are a deep purple colour and have a rich, sweet flavour making them excellent eaten fresh and as ingredients in cooking.

Finally come the blackberries – the sweet dark purple fruits of the bramble – which you can pick wild from the hedgerows from the end of August to mid-October. Old country superstition warns, though, that they should never be touched after old Michaelmas Day on 10 October, as on this day the devil is said to spit on the fruit to spite his rival, the Archangel Michael.

date and walnut loaf

A Scottish tea shop favourite.

you need

175 ml/6 fl oz/$^{3}/_{4}$ cup boiling water
125 g/4 oz/$^{3}/_{4}$ cup chopped dates
1 tsp bicarbonate of soda
125 g/4 oz/$^{5}/_{8}$ cup soft margarine
125 g/4 oz/$^{9}/_{16}$ cup caster sugar
1 large egg, beaten
250 g/9 oz/1$^{3}/_{4}$ cups plain flour
75 g/3 oz/$^{3}/_{4}$ cup walnut pieces
$^{1}/_{2}$ tsp vanilla extract

to make

Pour the boiling water over the dates and add the bicarbonate of soda. Leave to stand for 10 minutes. Pour the mixture into the breadmaker bucket, followed by the remaining ingredients. Fit the bucket into the breadmaker and set to the cake programme. After 5 minutes of the mixing cycle, scrape down the sides of the bucket with a plastic spatula to ensure all the ingredients are evenly mixed. When cooked, remove the bucket from the machine and leave to cool for 5 minutes. Carefully shake the loaf from the bucket and stand it the right way up on a wire cooling rack. Leave to cool.

black bun

This traditional Scottish recipe – also known as the Scotch Bun – is often served as a celebration cake around Hogmanay. In this unusual recipe a mixture of alcohol and spiced fruit is mashed into sweet dough, then wrapped in a plain piece of dough – keeping the bun moist during baking.

you need

225 ml/8 fl oz/1 cup full cream milk
175 ml/6 fl oz/$\frac{3}{4}$ cup melted butter
$\frac{1}{2}$ tsp salt
2 tbsp granulated sugar
450 g/16 oz/3 cups strong white bread flour
2$\frac{1}{2}$ tsp instant or fast-acting dried yeast

For the filling:

75 g/3 oz/$\frac{1}{2}$ cup currants
75 g/3 oz/$\frac{1}{2}$ cup raisins
75 g/3 oz/$\frac{3}{8}$ cup stoned and chopped ready to eat prunes
75 g/3 oz/$\frac{1}{2}$ cup stoned and chopped ready to eat dates
50 g/2 oz/$\frac{1}{2}$ cup flaked almonds
25 ml/1 fl oz/$\frac{1}{8}$ cup Scottish whisky
3 tbsp Dundee marmalade
1 tsp ground cinnamon
1 tsp ground cloves
1 tsp ground ginger
$\frac{1}{2}$ tsp ground cardamom

For the glaze:

1 medium egg yolk
1 tbsp full cream milk

to make

Lightly grease a baking tray. To make the dough, put the milk, butter, salt and sugar into the bread-maker bucket. Cover the mixture with the flour and finally sprinkle the yeast over the top. Fit the bucket into the breadmaker and set to the dough programme. To make the filling, mix the filling ingredients together in a bowl. Cover with film and leave to one side to allow the fruit to take up the flavour from the whisky. When the dough cycle is complete, turn the dough out on to a lightly floured surface. Cut away one third of the dough and set aside. Roll out the remaining two-thirds of dough into a large circle. Pile the filling ingredients into the centre of the circle and bring the dough up around the fruit and push together. Knead the dough to incorporate the fruit mixture. This is a messy job, but don't be too fussy – it should be sticky. Form the dough into a round about the size of a large tea plate and leave to rest. Roll out the remaining third of dough into a large circle. Place the fruited dough in the centre, bring the edges of the plain dough around and press the edges firmly together to seal. Turn the bun upside down to hide the edges and place on to the baking sheet. Cover with a tea towel and leave in a warm place to prove until doubled in size. To make the glaze, whisk together the egg yolk and milk. Brush the bun with the glaze and bake in a preheated oven at 200°C/400°F/gas mark 6 for 30 minutes until golden. When cooked, the loaf will sound hollow when tapped underneath.

ode to oats

The history of Scottish food has been greatly influenced by the Celtic traditions that were developed to sustain the needs of hard working communities. This, with the harsh climate and structure of the landscape, meant that oats, a hardy crop, flourished. Not surprisingly, therefore, oats are a staple of the Scottish diet and were traditionally used in cakes, bread, soups and porridge.

Harvested oat grains that have been cleaned and hulled are called grouts. Pinhead oats are grouts that have been cut into two or three pieces. Finer still is oatmeal, available generally in medium and fine ground varieties, with oat flour being the finest milled oat product.

Rolled oat grains are the usual ingredient for porridge and can also be used in bread and cakes for added texture. Oats and oatmeal absorb water quickly and easily from a dough mix and so recipes using these ingredients require a greater liquid content than standard wheat loaves.

oat and berry bread

Choose some of Scotland's finest soft fruit (see page 157) to make this tasty bread. The addition of oats makes this sustaining loaf perfect for breakfast.

you need

150 ml/5 fl oz/$^{5}/_{8}$ cup natural yogurt
150 ml/5 fl oz/$^{5}/_{8}$ cup water
2 tbsp granulated sugar
2 tsp salt
100 g/3$^{1}/_{2}$ oz/1 cup jumbo rolled oats
150g/5$^{1}/_{4}$ oz/1 cup fresh blueberries (or tayberries, blackberries or raspberries, if desired)
70 g/2$^{1}/_{2}$ oz/$^{1}/_{2}$ cup rye flour
150 g/5$^{1}/_{4}$ oz/1 cup soft grain white bread flour
225 g/8 oz/1$^{1}/_{2}$ cups very strong white bread flour
1$^{1}/_{2}$ tsp instant or fast-acting dried yeast

to make

Pour the yogurt and water into the breadmaker bucket, followed by the sugar, salt and oats. Add half the berries and cover the mixture with the flours. Finally sprinkle the yeast over the top. Fit the bucket into the breadmaker and set to the basic white programme. Add the remaining berries according to your manual's instructions, usually at the beginning of the second kneading cycle or when the machine bleeps. Once cooked, carefully shake the loaf from the bucket and stand it the right way up on a wire cooling rack. Leave the bread to cool for at least an hour before slicing and/or removing the paddle if necessary.

orkney broonies

Scotland has always enjoyed strong relations with Norway and in Edinburgh and Kirkwall on Orkney, Norwegian Constitution Day is often celebrated. In Kirkwall the celebrations include a parade through the Orkney town's centre with dancing in the evening. Orkney Broonies are served at such a celebration and are still eaten frequently on the island. For the breadmaker, I've made a single cake that can be quickly sliced into portions and served in pieces reminiscent of the original recipe. This sweet and robust cake flavoured with ginger and oatmeal is similar to parkin, though it's much lighter in texture which means that it can be enjoyed on the day that it's baked.

you need

225 g/8 oz/1½ cups fine oatmeal
125 g/4 oz/⅞ cup self raising flour
125 g/4 oz/½ cup margarine
125 ml/4 fl oz/½ cup buttermilk
1 large egg, beaten
150 g/5¼ oz/7/16 cup golden syrup
50 g/2 oz/⅛ cup black treacle
125 g/4 oz/¾ cup soft light brown sugar
2 tsp ground ginger
pinch of salt
½ tsp bicarbonate of soda

to make

Mix the oatmeal and flour together in a bowl and rub in the margarine with your fingertips until the mixture resembles fine breadcrumbs. Pour the buttermilk and egg into the breadmaker bucket, followed by the syrup and treacle. Cover the liquid with the flour mixture and finally add the sugar, ginger, salt and bicarbonate of soda. Fit the bucket into the breadmaker and set to the cake programme. After 5 minutes of the mixing cycle, scrape down the mixture on the sides of the bucket with a plastic spatula to ensure all the ingredients are evenly mixed. When cooked, remove the bucket from the machine and leave to cool for 5 minutes. Carefully shake the loaf from the bucket and stand it the right way up on a wire cooling rack. Leave to cool.

bannocks galore

Bannocks are simply round, flat loaves traditionally cooked on a griddle, but now commonly baked in the oven. Most Scottish towns had their own individual recipes and celebration bannocks were also made for special festivals and feasts. Today, the term bannock is used in a generic sense, with many books using it simply to describe a Scottish bread.

selkirk bannock

It's said that a baker authentically named Robbie Douglas first made the Selkirk Bannock in the mid-19th century. Enriched with milk, butter and fruit, it is likely that this loaf was first made as celebration bread.

you need

150 ml/5 fl oz/$^{5}/_{8}$ cup full cream milk
4 tbsp water
50 ml/2 fl oz/$^{1}/_{4}$ cup melted butter
50 ml/2 fl oz/$^{1}/_{4}$ cup sunflower oil
75g/3 oz/$^{5}/_{16}$ cup granulated sugar
1 tsp salt
450 g/16 oz/3 cups strong white bread flour
2 tsp instant or fast-acting dried yeast
150 g/5$^{1}/_{4}$ oz/1 cup sultanas

For the glaze:
1 tbsp milk
1 tbsp sugar

to make

Pour the milk, water, butter and oil into the breadmaker bucket. Add the sugar and salt and cover the mixture with the flour. Finally sprinkle the yeast over the top. Fit the bucket into the breadmaker and set to the basic white programme. Add the sultanas according to your manual's instructions, usually at the beginning of the second kneading cycle or when the machine bleeps. To make the glaze, whisk together the milk and sugar. Forty-five minutes before the end of the cycle, quickly lift the lid of the breadmaker and carefully brush on the glaze. Once cooked, carefully shake the loaf from the bucket and stand it the right way up on a wire cooling rack. Leave the bread to cool for at least an hour before slicing and/or removing the paddle if necessary.

the national drink

Whisky is the national drink of Scotland and the name itself comes from the Gaelic word *uisge beatha* meaning water of life. Whisky was produced illicitly throughout the Highlands and Islands for many hundreds of years and it is only since the mid-19th century that it became a commercial enterprise.

Two kinds of whisky are made in Scotland – malt and grain. Malt whiskies, still most frequently made in the Highlands and Islands, are generally made from barley only and are particularly sought after because of their distinctive bouquet and flavour. By contrast, grain whisky is made all over Scotland, from a mix of malted and unmalted grain. It is distilled in a continuous process and therefore does not have the subtleties of taste synonymous with malt whiskies. Once mature, grain whisky is blended using anything from 15 to 50 varieties in any one blend. Some single, unblended varieties are also sold although these are not so readily available.

atholl brose bread

Atholl Brose is a traditional Scottish tipple made from oats, honey and whisky – which some accredit to The Earl of Atholl in the 15th century. It may, however, be named simply after the district of the same name which occupies mostly mountainous country in highland Perth and Kinross – from Rannoch Moor in the west, Glen Isla in the east and to the River Almond in the south.

you need

8 tbsp fine oatmeal
450 ml/16 fl oz/2 cups water
2 tbsp whisky
2 tbsp sunflower oil
3 tbsp runny heather honey
1½ tsp salt
450 g/16 oz/3 cups very strong white bread flour
2½ tsp instant or fast-acting dried yeast

to make

Put 4 tbsp of the oatmeal into a jug and pour over the water. Stir and leave to soak for 30 minutes. Strain the oatmeal, reserving the liquid. Pour 225 ml/8 fl oz/1 cup of the oatmeal liquid into the breadmaker bucket. Discard the remaining liquor and soaked oatmeal. Add the whisky, oil, honey and salt. Cover the mixture with the flour, the remaining oatmeal and sprinkle the yeast over the top. Fit the bucket into the breadmaker and set to the basic white programme. Once cooked, carefully shake the loaf from the bucket and stand it the right way up on a wire cooling rack. Leave the bread to cool for at least an hour before slicing and/or removing the paddle if necessary.

heather honey and whisky bread

Mist-laden Scottish hills covered in rich, purple heather have become one of the best-known images of the country. In fact, heather is steeped in Scottish tradition – it's been used to make besoms to sweep floors, to make beds for hardy Highlanders and to bind around the battle staff used by the clan Macdonald. More famous today, however, is Scotland's rich and tangy heather honey that is thankfully now available nationwide. Used in this bread this unique honey adds a new dimension: a rich zing that shouts out over the warm undertones of Scottish malt whisky. I tried this bread with the smooth Macallan and the more peaty Bowmore, and my husband (a malt drinker) insists he could detect the individual nuances in both the loaves. Whatever whisky you choose, you're guaranteed a moist and flavoursome loaf that is perfect for both sweet and savoury accompaniments – it's delicious served with honey and jam, or cold meat and cheese.

you need

225 ml/8 fl oz/1 cup water
50 ml/2 fl oz/1/4 cup Scottish malt whisky
1 large egg yolk
3 tbsp melted butter
75 g/3 oz/3/16 cup runny heather honey
1 1/2 tsp salt
50 g/2 oz/1/4 cup fine oatmeal
100 g/3 1/2 oz/3/4 cup strong wholemeal flour
300 g/11 oz/2 cups very strong white bread flour
2 1/2 tsp instant or fast-acting dried yeast

to make

Pour the water, whisky, egg, butter and honey into the breadmaker bucket. Add the salt and cover the mixture with the oatmeal and the flour. Finally sprinkle the yeast over the top. Fit the bucket into the breadmaker and set to the basic white programme. Once cooked, carefully shake the loaf from the bucket and stand it the right way up on a wire cooling rack. Leave the bread to cool for at least an hour before slicing and/or removing the paddle if necessary.

TROUBLESHOOTING

Breadmakers and their owners are not infallible. So, if your loaves don't turn out as you'd hoped, use the notes below to guide you through the most common problems. See also the important recipe notes on pages 170–1.

PROBLEMS WHEN THE BREAD IS MIXING AND KNEADING

The Problem: The machine is running but the mixture is dry, crumbly and does not form a soft ball.
The Reason: Not enough liquid in the mix.
What to do: Add more liquid, 1 tbsp at a time during the kneading cycle until a soft dough is formed. Make sure you allow enough time for the dough to come together before adding more liquid.

The Problem: Dough is very sticky or runny and does not come together to form a ball.
The Reason: The dough is too wet.
What to do: Add a little flour, 1 tbsp at a time during the kneading cycle, waiting for the flour to be fully absorbed before adding more.

The Problem: The dough has not mixed or is only partially mixed.
The Reason: Either you forgot to fit the paddle into the bucket or the paddle was not fixed properly into the shaft. Alternatively, the bucket was not correctly fitted into the machine.
What to do: Check the paddle is fitted correctly and that the bucket is fixed securely into the machine.

PROBLEMS WITH RISING

The Problem: The bread rose too much and is sticking to the lid of the machine.
The Reason: This could be due to the following reasons:
• There is too much yeast in the recipe.
What to do: Reduce the yeast by ¼ tsp next time.
• There is too much sugar, or sweet ingredients in the recipe.
What to do: Reduce the sweet ingredients in the recipe next time.
• You may have forgotten to add salt to the dough.
What to do: Add ingredients slowly, taking time to measure each one accurately.
• The recipe used may contain too much dough volume for the capacity of your machine.
What to do: Check the recipe quantities match the amount of flour recommended for a loaf in your manufacturer's handbook.

The Problem: The bread has not risen enough.
The Reason: This could be because of one or more of the following:
• There is not enough yeast in the dough. Or, the yeast may be inactive because it is out of date or it was killed off because the liquid was too hot when you added it to the bucket.
What to do: Check the use-by information on your packet of yeast and don't use partially opened sachets. Take care that your liquid is at room temperature or lukewarm when you add

it to the bucket. If in doubt, always add liquid at a cooler rather than a hotter temperature.

- The yeast and salt came into contact with each other prior to the dough mixing.

What to do: Ensure that the flour acts as a buffer between the yeast and other ingredients. Always add the ingredients in the order specified by your manufacturer (see also note on pages 8– 9).

- The programme you chose may not have given the bread sufficient time to rise.

What to do: Always select the programme recommended for the recipe – rapid programmes are not always suitable.

- No sugar or sweet ingredients were added.

What to do: For best results there should be some sugar in every recipe. Yeast needs some sugar to feed it. However, too much will retard the yeast.

- There was too much salt in the recipe.

What to do: Take care to ensure that you use the tsp measure rather than the tbsp measure on your plastic spoon and make sure you don't add the salt twice.

- You may have used an unsuitable flour.

What to do: Unless stated in the recipe, always use strong flour for making bread (see notes on pages 11–13). Remember also that bread made with heavier flours like wholemeal and rye will not rise as high as their white equivalents and unless they are mixed with strong white flour, will not produce satisfactory loaves in a breadmaker.

- The dough was too dry. If this was the case it would not rise properly.

What to do: Always check your dough during the kneading cycles and make any adjustments necessary (see notes on dry and wet mixes on opposite page).

The Problem: The bread did not rise at all.

The Reason: No yeast was added. Or, the yeast added was either inactive, killed off by other ingredients by being too hot, or, was past its sell-by date.

What to do: Take care when adding ingredients, it's easy to miss something out. Also, make sure that your ingredients are within their sell-by date and that liquids are added at the correct temperature.

The Problem: The bread has collapsed after rising or during baking.

The Reason: This could be because of one or more of the following:

- The dough was too wet.

What to do: Either reduce the liquid by 1–2 tbsp next time or add a little more flour.

- There was too much yeast in the mixture.

What to do: Reduce the amount of yeast slightly next time.

- Not enough salt was added to control the action of the yeast.

What to do: Check the amount of salt in the recipe.

- High humidity or warm weather may have caused the dough to collapse for no apparent reason.

What to do: See notes on page 10.

- The dough may have contained a high proportion of cheese or too much fresh onion or garlic.

What to do: See notes on page 16.

PROBLEMS WITH BAKING

The Problem: There is smoke coming from the machine and a smell of burning.
The reason: Either the ingredients or the dough have been spilt onto the heating element.
What to do: Always add the ingredients to the bucket when the bucket is out of the machine. Take care when adding ingredients during the kneading cycles not to spill them down the edge of the bucket. Wipe the machine out with a damp cloth once it is cold.

The Problem: The bread has mixed but not baked.
The Reason: You may have selected the dough cycle by accident.
What to do: Either remove the dough from the bucket and bake in the oven, or select the 'bake' cycle to finish the bread, if your machine offers this function.

The Problem: The bread is not baked in the centre or on top.
The Reason: This could be for any of the following reasons.
• The dough was too wet.
What to do: Add less liquid and check the dough when mixing, making any necessary adjustments during the kneading cycle.
• The quantities for the recipe were too much for your machine and it could not bake the loaf effectively.
What to do: Check the maximum amount of flour recommended in your manufacturer's handbook and ensure any recipe you choose does not exceed this amount.
• The dough was too rich. It may have contained too much fat, sugar or eggs.
What to do: Check the recipe and reduce quantities of the above ingredients slightly.

PROBLEMS WITH FINISHED LOAVES

The Problem: The crust is shrivelled or wrinkled.
The Reason: Moisture has condensed on the top of the cooked loaf.
What to do: Remove the bread from the machine as soon as the cycle has finished.

The Problem: There are deposits of flour on the sides of the loaf.
The Reason: Sometimes dry ingredients stick to the sides of the pan during kneading and then stick unmixed to the risen dough.
What to do: Check the dough while it is mixing and, if necessary, carefully scrape down the mixture on the sides of the bucket with a plastic spatula to ensure all the ingredients are evenly mixed.

The Problem: The bread has a crumbly, coarse texture.
The Reason: Either, the bread rose too much or the dough was too dry.
What to do: Either reduce the amount of yeast slightly next time or add more liquid to make a more pliable dough.

The Problem: The loaf has a burnt crust.
The Reason: There could be too much sugar in the dough or the dark setting was wrongly selected.
What to do: Use less sugar or try the 'light' crust setting next time. The sweet

bread setting will also be better for producing a lighter crust.

The Problem: The loaf is very pale.
The Reason: The ingredients in the recipe may not encourage browning. Or, the particular recipe may require a longer baking time to make a better crust.
What to do: This can be remedied by one of the following:
- Add milk, either dried or fresh, to the dough as this encourages browning.
- Select the dark crust option if your machine has one.
- Increase the sugar content slightly.
- Experiment with different glazes. Milk and beaten egg will help encourage a golden crust.

The Problem: The crust is tough and chewy.
The Reason: There was too little or no fat in the recipe.
What to do: Increase the fat content by adding a little more butter, fat, oil or milk.

The Problem: The added ingredients were chopped up instead of remaining whole.
The Reason: Delicate ingredients were added at the beginning of the cycle.
What to do: Add ingredients such as fruit and nuts when the machine bleeps or towards the end of the second kneading cycle (see the instructions in your manual). Also, try leaving fruit and nuts in larger pieces.

The Problem: The added ingredients were not mixed in properly.
The Reason: The ingredients were added too late in the kneading cycle.
What to do: Follow the instructions in your manual or add the ingredients a little earlier.

The Problem: The bread is too dry.
The Reason: The bread was left, uncovered, to cool for too long and has dried out or the bread has been stored in the fridge.
What to do: When cooling bread, wrap it in a cloth or a tea towel and only store bread after it has cooled. Bread is best stored in a clean, dry cloth or in a plastic bag and kept in a cool, dry place, not in the fridge.

The Problem: The bread has a holey texture.
The Reason: Either the dough was too wet or the salt was omitted from the dough. Bear in mind that warm weather or high humidity can also cause the dough to rise too quickly.
What to do: Ensure salt is added to the mix and check the dough while mixing to guarantee the right consistency.

The Problem: The bread is difficult to cut and squashes easily when sliced. The slices are doughy and tacky.
The Reason: Either the bread was cut straight away after being baked or was not allowed sufficient time to cool before slicing.
What to do: Allow the bread to cool completely before attempting to slice it.

Remember that you are making homemade bread. You don't have to produce standard, uniform loaves each time. Instead, give yourself realistic expectations and enjoy the fact that every loaf will be different. Breadmakers will produce delicious breads, it may just take a little practice.

RECIPE NOTES AND CONVERSION CHARTS

The conversions below are for flour only and are based on the 225 ml/8 fl oz plastic cup measure supplied with most bread machines. These conversions will not be applicable to other dry ingredients, as 1 cup of flour will weigh a different amount from 1 cup of walnuts or 1 cup of grated cheese. Therefore, the chart below should only be used for flour.

Flour Conversions Only

25 g	1 oz	
50 g	2 oz	
70 g	2½ oz	½cup
75 g	3 oz	⅝ cup
100 g	3 ½ oz	¾ cup
125 g	4 oz	⅞ cup
150 g	5 ¼ oz	1 cup
175 g	6 oz	
190 g	6½ oz	1¼ cups
200 g	7 oz	
225 g	8 oz	1 ½ cups
250 g	9 oz	1 ¾ cups
275 g	10 oz	
300 g	11 oz	2 cups
350 g	12 oz	
375 g	13 oz	2 ½ cups
400 g	14 oz	2 ¾ cups
425 g	15oz	
450 g	16 oz/1 lb	3 cups
475 g	17oz	
500 g	17 ½ oz	3 ½ cups
525 g	18 ½ oz	
550 g	19 ½ oz	
575 g	20 oz	3 ⅞ cups
600 g	21 oz	4 cups

Liquid Conversions Only

25 ml	1 fl oz	1/8 cup
50 ml	2 fl oz	1/4 cup
75 ml	3 fl oz	3/8 cup
125 ml	4 fl oz	1/2 cup
150 ml	5 fl oz	5/8 cup
175 ml	6 fl oz	3/4 cup
200 ml	7 fl oz	7/8 cup
225 ml	8 fl oz	1 cup
250 ml	9 fl oz	1 1/8 cups
275 ml	10 fl oz	1 1/4 cups
300 ml	11 fl oz	1 3/8 cups
350 ml	12 fl oz	1 1/2 cups
375 ml	13 fl oz	1 5/8 cups
400 ml	14 fl oz	1 3/4 cups
425 ml	15 fl oz	1 7/8 cups
450 ml	16 fl oz	2 cups

IMPORTANT NOTES

Measure ingredients carefully. Take time to let liquid settle in the measure and read from the side on a level surface. For flour, tap the cup lightly to level the surface, but do not squash the flour or other ingredients into the cup.

Always use the plastic spoon measure supplied with your bread machine. Never use household cutlery as these vary greatly in capacity and can lead to inaccurate measuring of ingredients and poor results.

If you prefer to use grams and ounces, I would recommend investing in a set of digital scales to measure ingredients for your breadmaking. Most of these scales will measure both wet and dry ingredients.

Use one set of measures only; never mix metric, imperial or cups in the same recipe.

Always check that the total amount of flour in a recipe is the same as the total amount recommended in your manufacturer's handbook. If your machine makes different sizes of loaf, check which setting is applicable for the chosen recipe.

FLOUR, YEAST & INGREDIENTS

Allinson
Flour and yeast
Allinson Baking Club
0870 240 2237
www.bakingmad.com

Claybrooke Mill
01455 202443

Doves Farm
Speciality flours
01488 684 880
www.dovesfarm.co.uk

REGIONAL SPECIALITIES

Food From Britain
www.foodfrombritain.co.uk
a web site with links to regional food initiatives and specialist suppliers

Northern Ireland Food and Drink Association
www.nifda.co.uk

Regional Farm Shops
www.farmshopping.com
www.bigbarn.co.uk

Regional Farmers' Markets
www.farmersmarkets.net
for information on your nearest farmers' market

CHEESE SPECIALISTS

Web Sites Selling British Regional Cheeses:
www.cheese2please.co.uk
www.chestercheeseshop.com
www.houseofcheese.co.uk
www.picnic-fayre.co.uk
www.inverawe.co.uk

Other useful Cheese contacts:
The Cheese Society
01522 511003
www.thecheesesociety.co.uk

Cropwell Bishop Creamery
0115 989 2350
www.cropwellbishopstilton.com

The Fine Cheese Company
01225 448748
www.finecheese.co.uk

Huge Cheese Direct
020 7819 6099
www.hugecheesedirect.co.uk

The Teddington Cheese
020 8940 1944
www.teddingtoncheese.co.uk

DRINK CONTACTS

Scottish Whisky
www.whisky-heritage.co.uk
www.whiskynet.co.uk

Irish Whiskey
www.classicwhiskey.com

Real Ale
www.camra.co.uk

Cider
www.ukcider.co.uk

BREAD MACHINE MANUFACTURERS

Electrolux (via Currys)
08701 545570
www.currys.co.uk

Morphy Richards
08450 777700
www.morphyrichards.com

Panasonic
08705 357357
www.panasonic.co.uk

Prima International
0113 251 1500
www.prima-international.com

Pulse Home Products Ltd
0161 621 6900
www.breville.co.uk

Russell Hobbs
0161 947 3000
www.russellhobbs.com

index

acknowledgements

Special thanks to:

My husband Simon, for his belief and support and for being such an excellent Dad to baby Finlay while Mummy was baking bread.

Sheila Watson, my agent, for her attention to detail and good humour.

Grace Cheetham from Ebury who, from the other side of the world, helped turn an acorn into an oak – bringing this book to fruition.